D0272636

THE ROYAL HORTICULTURAL SOCIETY COLLECTION

THE *wild flower* GARDEN

THE ROYAL HORTICULTURAL SOCIETY COLLECTION

THE *wild flower* GARDEN

NOËL KINGSBURY

BCA

LONDON NEW YORK SYDNEY TORONTO

This edition published 1994 by BCA by arrangement with Conran Octopus Limited.

First published in 1994 by Conran Octopus Limited
37 Shelton Street, London WC2H 9HN

Text and original planting schemes
copyright © Noël Kingsbury 1994

Design and layout copyright © Conran Octopus Limited 1994

The right of Noël Kingsbury to be identified as author of this
work has been asserted by him in accordance with the
Copyright, Designs and Patents Act 1988.

All rights reserved. No part of this book may be reproduced,
stored in a retrieval system, or transmitted in any form or by
any means, electronic, electrostatic, magnetic tape,
mechanical, photocopying, recording, or otherwise, without the
prior permission in writing of the publisher.

A catalogue record for this book is available from the
British Library.

ISBN 1 85029 539 5

Project Editor	Jane O'Shea
Project Art Editor	Ann Burnham
Editor	Carole McGlynn
Designer	Alistair Plumb
Picture Researcher	Helen Fickling
Editorial Assistant	Caroline Davison
Production	Sonya Sibbons
Illustrators	Lynn Chadwick
	Vanessa Luff
	Valerie Price
	Lesley Craig

CN5619

Typeset by Servis Filmsetting Ltd, England
Printed and bound in Hong Kong

FRONT JACKET *Poppies* (Papaver rhoeas) *with ox-eye
daisies* (Leucanthemum vulgare).

BACK JACKET *Tall plants in a mid-summer meadow
include ox-eye daisies and the red seedheads of
docks* (Rumex *species*).

PAGE 1 *Dog's tooth violet* (Erythronium dens-canis)
with primrose (Primula vulgaris).

PAGE 2 *Red campion* (Silene dioica) *with meadow
cranesbill* (Geranium pratensis) *and valerian foliage*
(Centranthus ruber).

RIGHT *Cowslips* (Primula veris) *in short grass line
a path between a naturalized planting of narcissi
and tulips.*

CONTENTS

WHAT IS WILD FLOWER GARDENING?

Wild flowers have a subtle beauty that is best appreciated if they are grown blended and intermingled as they would be in nature, but this does not mean that it is essential to have vast acres of woodland or meadow before you can enjoy growing wild plants. Indeed, wild flowers can be grown in traditional garden settings in towns and suburbs as well as in the country. Colourful meadow flowers, for example, can be grown alongside garden plants in a flower bed, as well as in a wild meadow garden, and many types of spring bulb can be grown around individual trees and shrubs, to increase steadily year after year.

Colourful cornfield annuals make a quick and easy introduction to wild flower gardening: cornflower (Centaurea cyanus), corn poppy (Papaver rhoeas) and corn chamomile (Anthemis arvensis) flower within months of sowing. Cornfield wild flowers are one of the most colourful spectacles when in flower, but they are short-lived. Permanent wild flower plantings must involve perennial species that last from year to year.

7

Prairie coneflower (Echinacea purpurea) *is an excellent nectar source for butterflies, in this case a tiger swallowtail.*

Kingcups (Caltha palustris) *and skunk cabbage* (Lysichiton americanus) *are two early flowering and rapidly naturalizing wild flowers for damp places, creating an easily-maintained wild area in a traditional garden.*

A wild flower garden is a garden inspired by nature, where the emphasis is on growing plant species that occur in the wild in an informal and natural-looking way. It is not a garden left to run wild, nor is it necessarily an imitation of nature, but a place where the art and control of the gardener are tempered by a consciousness of natural plant associations and habits of growth. The wild flower gardener works with nature, by planting only what will grow in the existing conditions of soil and site – most wild flowers do not need fertilizer and will flourish in poor soil. The gardener can guide things in the right direction but will then leave nature to play its part; in time, self-seeding will help to create an informal, naturalistic effect that could never be achieved by rigorous planning and soil improvements alone.

Wild flowers can be incorporated in both town and country gardens in different ways: a wild flower garden does not have to be wild. Without altering the basic layout of a traditional garden, without encroaching on the trimness of the lawn or the order of its flower beds, a wide selection of wild flowers can be successfully introduced in the beds and borders, to bring colour and interest to all seasons. On the other hand they can be grown in a setting that is much closer to the way they would grow in the wild and this is generally known as the wild garden. Both possibilities are explored further in the chapter on Wild flowers for all gardens, page 18.

Why grow wild flowers?

To our ancestors, struggling to maintain a few fields against the encroachment of the surrounding wilderness, the idea of cultivating a wild flower garden would have been a contradiction in terms. But today we live in a world where there is hardly any wilderness left. Many of the wild flowers familiar to our grandparents' generation have become a rare sight in our's, largely through the destruction of their natural habitats. Many gardeners feel a need to redress the balance by bringing some of these vanishing wild flowers into their gardens.

The wild flowers covering the ground in this olive grove – a species of iris and ox-eye daisies (Leucanthemum vulgare) – illustrate how plants often grow, in drifts rather than being distributed evenly.

In an increasingly urban world, people are beginning to see their gardens as islands of countryside, as oases for nature in the desert of the city or the vast, open spaces created by industrial agriculture. Many of us feel that we need the countryside or the wilderness for relaxation or for spiritual refreshment. We can escape to it for holidays or weekends, of course, but how much more enriching to have some, even if only a little bit, that is much nearer to hand. Growing wild flowers is one of the ways in which we can achieve this.

There are gardeners who are interested in making their gardens into havens for wildlife, and who wish to grow wild flowers in order to encourage butterflies, birds and other animals. Properly planned and managed, a wild garden can attract an enormous range of wildlife, which is an obvious boon for the naturalist, and a source of endless fascination for children. Nature thrives on diversity, so the wider the selection of wild flowers, shrubs and trees introduced into a garden, the better.

Some people have simply become dissatisfied with conventional gardens, seeing them as an environment that is too controlled, the plants growing in them too artificial, and involving considerable use of chemicals. There is a growing interest in a more relaxed style of garden, one that complements the environment rather than adding to its burdens, and wild flowers are very much a part of this new style.

Once established, a wild flower garden is low in maintenance and this is part of its appeal for gardeners who do not have time for the weeding, pruning, tidying, mowing and other tasks required by more conventional forms of gardening. Wild plants are used to surviving the competition of other flowers and grasses and can therefore be grown in quite a different way to garden flowers. Woodland plants and bulbs become naturalized, gradually spreading and multiplying, and a meadow planting may need no more than an annual cut.

A garden with a high proportion of wild flowers is also open to the possibility of nature adding more

A mix of wild flowers and cottage-garden annuals consort in this border in late summer. The tall yellow plant is a mullein (Verbascum species), the smaller yellow is mignonette (Reseda lutea). Mulleins are biennial but always self-sow well and thrive on light, dry soils, as does mignonette.

species. In an established wild garden, the numbers of species will also slowly increase over time, as the wind, birds and other animals introduce seeds of species not represented in the original planting. One of the most exciting aspects of the mature wild garden is a sense of partnership with nature and the satisfaction of nature reclaiming something for itself.

What is a wild flower?

Wild flowers are one of the most important elements in making up the images of the countryside that we love, whether drifts of springtime flowers in a woodland – bluebells, primroses, anemones – or the multicoloured haze of a meadow in summer – with clovers, cranesbills, vetches, knapweeds – or the luxuriant vegetation of a riverside, with irises, reeds, purple and yellow loosestrife. Until recently, there was little interest in growing wild flowers in gardens but now that this is changing, more and more gardeners wish to bring some of the countryside's natural beauty into their immediate surroundings.

A wild flower can be defined as any native species of flowering plant, but what most people understand by a wild flower is one that is herbaceous, dying

down to ground level in winter to re-emerge the following spring. In this book we will also look at low-growing and shrubby plants as well as ferns.

Many garden plants, by contrast, are 'cultivars', which indicates that they have been specially bred or selected for commercial reasons. A hybrid is a cross between two species; this can occur in the wild but is usually deliberately made to produce a unique plant with the best characteristics of both parents. Some cultivars are selections made from the wild, where a particular form of the species will have been chosen for commercial production because of special characteristics, such as colour or flower size. But other, more intensively bred cultivars and hybrids are quite unlike their remote progenitors in the wild. You would never come across a hedgerow of double roses, for instance, or a field of marigolds with huge heads.

A growing number of gardeners are finding that they prefer the natural beauty and delicacy of wild plants – the colours are softer, the flowers better proportioned and quite often the plants are tougher. But not all wild flowers are necessarily desirable. There are plenty that are vigorous, adaptable, opportunistic and yet, to the human eye, not very

ABOVE *The author, Noël Kingsbury, seen against a colourful wild hedgerow planting.*

RIGHT *Snake's-head fritillaries (Fritillaria meleagris) are among the first flowers of the year in this damp meadow. Their extraordinary chequer-patterned flowers and the ease with which they establish put them among the best wild flowers for such a site.*

Starry false solomon's seal (Smilacina stellata), *Phlox divaricata and lady fern* (Athyrium filix-femina) *make lush growth in a shady spot, photographed in spring. The phlox is a good ground cover, while the foliage of the other plants looks attractive throughout the summer.*

pleasing. In a traditional garden they would be classed as weeds and even in a wild garden they may be defined as such – a plant in the wrong place at the wrong time. Plants like thistles (*Cirsium*), docks (*Rumex*), stinging nettles (*Urtica diocia*) and certain grasses such as couch (*Agropyron repens*), can make it extremely difficult, or even impossible, to establish other, more attractive vegetation. This is not to say that these plants are without value; docks are an excellent seed source for small birds and nettles are vital for butterfly larvae. These vigorous plants can have their place, in less frequented corners of the garden for instance.

Growing native plants

For many people, a wild flower can be defined as such only if it is native to the region in which it is growing, and not from the other side of the world. Many gardens are planted with species originally introduced from far-flung parts of the globe, and yet there may be native species that are just as colourful, and often easier to grow, in the hedgerow down the road. Some plants that we think of as wild are in fact introductions from other countries and other regions that have integrated themselves so well into the local flora that we think of them as natives. Examples of

such plants include the beautiful clear blue flowers of chicory (*Cichorium intybus*) and wild carrot (*Daucus carota*), with their lacy white heads, that are so common by roadsides in the eastern USA as well as being a familiar feature of our own countryside. And if a few non-invasive 'new' plants are added to the local flora every now and again, so much the better. In some ways, this increasing diversity may be of great importance in years to come if the recent climatic changes prevail.

Part of the basic philosophy of wild flower gardening is to work with nature and to grow what thrives naturally on the site, rather than making extensive modifications in order to grow particular plants. Wild flowers and grasses as well as trees and shrubs that are native to a locality are adapted to local conditions, so that they will not need special irrigation, drainage, feeding or protecting. Growing plants from areas with very different climates in the garden, on the other hand, often means extra effort in keeping them happy. In fact much garden work is to do with trying to change conditions to suit the plants – gardeners with wet soil lay land drains so that lavender may grow; if dry, they irrigate so that irises will thrive; those with acid soil often add lime to grow better roses, while those with limy soils may add peat for rhododendrons. The wild flower gardener prefers to work the other way round, selecting those species that will thrive in the given conditions.

There are several reasons why we should not restrict ourselves totally to native species, however, and I am a great believer in mixing natives and non-native plants in wild flower gardening. The local wild flora can look drab at certain times of year; in many parts of Europe, late summer and autumn can be particularly difficult to fill with local wild-flower colour. Owners of small gardens and city gardens are often especially concerned to make the most of a limited space, which means there is no room for plants with only a brief season of interest. They may decide to use local wild flowers as only one element in a garden that also includes roses, early flowering shrubs or long-blooming bedding plants.

Lady's slipper orchid (Cypripedium acaule) is a wild flower that has suffered immensely from commercial collecting, like most orchids. Unfortunately it is not easy to establish in the garden, nor to propagate.

But beware! The danger with some non-native wild flowers is that they can show aggressive tendencies outside of their homeland and spread to become notorious as weeds. Any plant that is known for its exceptionally vigorous growth or rapid powers of reproduction should never be grown anywhere near open countryside where it could conceivably spread. Japanese knotweed (*Reynoutria japonica*) is a well known, and much hated, example of a plant that has been introduced into gardens in Europe and the USA, and escaped to become a major problem of undeveloped countryside. Indeed, it is illegal to introduce this and certain other alien species into the wild: in the United States, the cultivation of purple loosestrife (*Lythrum salicaria*) is banned because, although it is not especially invasive in its native Europe, it has proved to be so in American wetland. So if you are creating a wild garden in the country and you want to be adventurous, it is important to do some initial research into the species you are interested in planting; consider consulting your local agricultural advisory service or a conservation body such as the Nature Conservancy Council.

Even desirable wild flowers can sometimes become a problem on their home ground. An example is the European ox-eye daisy (*Leucanthemum vulgare*), a showy and easily established mid-summer wild flower. On fertile soils it may grow so strongly that it can smother smaller, less vigorous wild flower species. Controlling the growth of such potential menaces is one of the essential tasks in creating wild gardens, and is covered in the chapter on Establishing wild flower habitats, page 69.

Wild flower growing and conservation

Until recently, it was the general practice for large numbers of wild plants to be dug from the wild for sale to the gardening public. Unfortunately, many of these were the kind of plant that is least able to reproduce quickly to replace its losses, and in some cases the commercial digging up of plants has resulted in localized extinctions. Orchids have been badly affected, the slipper orchids (*Cypripedium* species) having been decimated throughout Europe and North America. The tragedy is that wild orchids do not transplant easily and the majority of the plants dug up do not survive in gardens. Other slow-growing woodland plants such as trilliums and bloodroot (*Sanguinaria*) have also been targets for commercial collecting.

Nature is not a bottomless resource that can be plundered at will, and the vast majority of gardeners will appreciate how harmful the collecting of wild plants is. There are certain conservation guidelines that most wild flower gardeners will be only too happy to follow:

• Do not collect plants from the wild, except as part of a rescue operation which is best organized by a local conservation body.

• If you collect seeds from the wild, take only limited quantities and only from locally abundant species. The same applies to cutting material.

• Buy wild flowers or bulbs only from companies that declare their origin to be 'nursery propagated' (not just 'nursery grown'). If you have any doubts, ask some searching questions about their origins.

• Be especially careful when buying known rarities or species that are commonly collected in the wild, such as orchids or trilliums. If in doubt, do not buy.

13

WILD FLOWERS FOR ALL GARDENS

Some gardeners want a totally 'wild' garden, for which wild flowers are the obvious choice, but there are other gardeners who, for reasons of limited space or personal preference, want to have borders and lawns and a much trimmer look, yet who still wish to enjoy the natural beauty of wild flowers. There is no reason at all why they should not have them. In this chapter we look at the different ways in which all kinds of garden can be planned to include wild flowers.

Beyond the trim lawn, an area of spring meadow around some fruit trees lends an informal beauty to this garden. Here sheep's parsley (Anthriscus sylvestris), *daisies* (Bellis perennis) and meadow buttercups (Ranunculus acris) grow among a variety of grasses. Earlier in the season naturalized daffodils were a feature of this meadow area. After midsummer the meadow will be cut and kept to no more than 10cm (4in) for the rest of the year.

Opportunities for growing wild flowers

An early-morning mist enshrouds a meadow in this country garden. Some wild garden plantings, particularly meadows, can appear untidy after the mid-summer flowers have finished, but ox-eye daisies (Leucanthemum vulgare) will flower quite late into the season, contrasting with the red seedheads of docks (Rumex species).

Gardeners who want to grow wild flowers are often drawn to them by the sight of swathes of meadow flowers or areas of woodland where spring flowers cover the ground in sheets. But wild flowers can equally well be grown in smaller and more conventional garden settings, even within the layout of formal gardens or the high walls of urban backyards.

In planning to include wild flowers in your garden you will need to ask yourself how wild you want to be. Do you want to grow wild flowers exclusively, or do you want to grow them alongside more traditional garden plants? Do you want a totally wild garden, or a wild area or two within your garden, or would you prefer to grow wild flowers within a framework of beds and borders? The size of the garden has a significant bearing on the level at which you incorporate wild flowers. Gardeners who tend a small plot will often want to maintain a conventional

and orderly format of lawn and borders with the reliability of colour and the tidy growth of traditional garden plants. The totally wild garden is not for them. The main problem in small plots is that a wild garden can so easily appear simply uncared for, and can look out of place when seen alongside neighbouring gardens. These gardeners will be more interested in how to include wild flowers in borders, among shrubs, on rock gardens and in containers.

In medium-sized or larger gardens, of 500 square metres (an eighth of an acre) and above, there is scope to include a little more wilderness. There should be enough room to incorporate a small wild area – a piece of meadow, for instance, or a wetland area next to a pond, or a woodland planting underneath some trees. But such an area will have to be carefully planned, so that it fits in well with the rest of the garden. The planting will also have to be appropriate

for the conditions of the site, so that the wild flowers chosen will be those that naturally grow in the type of soil, the levels of light and the degree of moisture.

There is no doubt that wild gardens work best visually on a large scale. Those with gardens of over 2,000 square metres (half an acre or more), especially in the country, will have exciting opportunities to create more extensive wild areas. It is important that country gardens appear to be an established part of the surrounding countryside as inappropriate plantings can ruin a landscape almost as much as unsympathetic buildings. An example would be the tall, dark leyland cypress (× *Cupressocyparis leylandii*) which so often obtrudes in a country landscape of deciduous trees, fields and hedgerows. Later in this chapter we look at how the use of wild flowers and native trees and shrubs can do much to integrate a garden into the country landscape.

Those who garden in towns, cities and even the suburbs may, on the other hand, need to screen themselves off from their intrusive urban surroundings and create a sense of privacy in their gardens. Wild flowers can do much to help recreate a country atmosphere and will be a refreshing influence even in an oppressively built-up environment.

Planning to incorporate wild flowers

Whatever the size of the garden, wherever it is, or however wild it is, certain considerations will have to be borne in mind at an early stage of planning. A key factor is seasonal interest. Owners of small gardens in particular, or where parts of the garden are highly visible all the time, will want as much as possible to look at all year round. Others may only use the garden in summer, and so will be primarily concerned with a colourful display of flowers for those months. The garden's appearance outside the main flowering season must also be a consideration; what is seen by some as the natural beauty of seedheads blowing in the breeze, will be viewed by other eyes as unkempt and uncared-for grass.

The uses of a garden must also be considered. Is it mainly for looking at or strolling through, or will it

be used more intensively? Families with children can make quite heavy demands on a garden – young children will need areas of short, hard-wearing grass for playing games, for example.

The level of maintenance required is another consideration. One advantage of wild gardens is that, once established, they require relatively little maintenance, which of course makes them admirably suited to those with little time or energy for gardening tasks such as weeding, staking and pruning. But all garden plantings will demand more time and attention while they establish themselves than when they are mature. Above all they will need weeding, to remove those unwanted plants that threaten to overwhelm the chosen species. Some kinds of wild flower planting need a lot more maintenance until they establish than others; for example a chalk downland will require more work than a wetland area. And wild flower meadows need sensitive and careful maintenance in their first few years. In particular they need frequent cutting, in order to restrict the growth of the more tenacious grasses like timothy (*Phleum pratense*) and vigorous wild flower species like yarrow (*Achillea millefolium*).

In these attractively informal borders, the wild plants have been allowed to intermingle with garden plants and choose where they want to grow. This kind of planting looks entirely appropriate in a conventional garden, however small, provided it is informal in style. The pinky-red valerian (Centranthus ruber) in the foreground is a wild flower that spreads easily but not rampantly; it is especially good on dry or stony soils.

Incorporating wild flowers in borders

The relaxed growth of bright pink cranesbill (Geranium endressii) and hedge woundwort (Stachys sylvatica) make a good juxtaposition with the formal shape of these conifers. Wild flowers can be used effectively to make such contrasts with formal garden features. The cranesbill will carry on flowering for most of the summer.

Wild flowers may be grown in beds and borders in much the same way as traditional garden plants, and this can be the easiest way to incorporate them in small gardens. The dividing line between wild flowers and garden plants is often a narrow one – after all, many garden plants are identical to their wild ancestors – and there is no reason why many more wild flowers cannot be introduced to the border.

The plants commonly grown in gardens have been chosen for such characteristics as compact habit and a long flowering season. Garden plants have also been selected for their ability to concentrate strong colours in a small area, which is what makes a flower garden so intensely colourful compared to plants growing naturally in the wild. Many wild flowers do not behave in quite the predictable fashion that gardeners like, which limits their usefulness in a well-ordered garden. But the rather unkempt nature of some wild flowers and the tendency of some to self-seed over paths matters far less in an informal garden. And while the more muted colours and sparser flowering habits of wild flowers do not appeal to everybody, the emphasis on restraint, the subtle beauty of the flowers and the apparent insouciance of the planting are aspects of wild flowers that make them admirable subjects for a relaxed style of garden.

Nevertheless, there are many wild flowers that have all the characteristics of good border plants, although they have never been seriously cultivated in gardens (see the list on page 25) and it is these wild flowers that fit most easily into traditional gardening schemes. However common they are in the wild, they can introduce a note of novelty into the garden, simply because people are not used to seeing them in a border. Even those wild flowers that are less obvious as border plants need not be excluded. If a wild flower has a short period of flower, for instance, this will not matter greatly if it is surrounded in the border by long-flowering cultivated plants.

Choosing wild flowers to grow with garden plants

The key to success in choosing wild flowers for the border lies in selecting those that will be compatible with your garden plants and, ideally, which also enhance them. Wild flowers in a border either need to be showy enough not to be outshone by colourful garden plants, like the red campion (*Silene dioica*) whose glorious pink flowers last for most of spring, or the vivid purple clustered bellflower (*Campanula glomerata*), or they need to make other, more subtle contributions to the border. An example of the latter might be the elegant seedheads of the teasel (*Dipsacus fullonum*) that can be appreciated right through the depths of winter. Another suggestion would be to grow sweet cicely (*Myrrhis odorata*) next to some showy astilbe cultivars. They will both thrive in a slightly shaded border, the ferny foliage and subtle white 'cow-parsley' flowers of the sweet cicely forming a backdrop for the stronger form and colour of the astilbe. Once both have finished flowering, the mahogany brown seedpods of sweet cicely will provide an additional focus of interest.

RIGHT *In this garden ferns such as the male fern* (Dryopteris filix-mas) *and hart's tongue* (Phyllitis scolopendrium) *have been encouraged to spread themselves among rock-garden plants like erodiums and thymes.*

BELOW *This vibrant border at the foot of a wall shows how colourful wild flowers can be: foxgloves* (Digitalis purpurea), *dame's violet* (Hesperis matronalis), *buttercups* (Ranunculus arvensis), *heartsease* (Viola tricolor) *and corn marigold* (Chrysanthemum segetum).

as camellia and rhododendron (if the soil is acid) and herbaceous plants such as astilbe and hosta. In the larger border there may be a place for wild flowers that are vigorous spreaders such as yellow archangel (*Lamiastrum galeobdolon*) and enthusiastic self-seeders such as lesser celandine (*Ranunculus ficaria*), but they may overwhelm a smaller border. Provided it stays under control, however, self-seeding can be a welcome asset, as a few randomly placed flower spikes can give an informal and carefree look to the smallest border. On neutral to acid soils, foxgloves (*Digitalis purpurea*) are especially good at responsible self-seeding, their tall, narrow spires of mauve-pink flowers rarely getting in the way of other plants. On more alkaline soils, nettle-leaved bellflower (*Campanula trachelium*) and the giant bellflower (*C. latifolia*), with spikes of purple flowers, can fulfil a similar role.

A more practical aspect of compatibility is the problem posed by the rather invasive habits of some wild flowers, which come to the fore when they do not have the restraining influence of close companions as they would do in the wild. This does not

Some wild flowers bloom in a blaze of glory and then, like a firework, return quickly to obscurity, while others can be guaranteed to provide months of colour. The smaller the garden or the space, the more plants you will want in the latter category, for instance some of the pink hardy cranesbills like *Geranium endressii* or *G. versicolor*. Many late-summer meadow species last a long time in flower too, such as knapweeds (*Centaurea*) and yarrow (*Achillea*).

Those keen to attract wildlife to the garden may well want to include in their borders wild flowers that are not so showy, but that have importance for particular animals and insects. For example, a few plants of the unexciting looking hedge-garlic (*Alliaria petiolata*) will not detract too much from a border, but will provide an important food source for caterpillars of the European orange tip butterfly.

You may wish to consider adding wild flowers to a mixed border in half shade, where there is sunlight for up to half the day, to plant alongside shrubs such

matter too much if all the plants you are growing together are vigorous and able to stand up for themselves, but weaker species might be rapidly swamped. Some wild flowers seed themselves around with gay abandon, like ragged robin (*Lychnis flos-cuculi*) or jacob's ladder (*Polemonium caeruleum*), while others have root systems that are always sending up new plants at a distance from the parent, such as tansy (*Tanacetum officinale*) or canada goldenrod (*Solidago canadense*). These habits might be welcome in the wild garden, or in a very informal border, but they can mean extra maintenance in a small and tidy one. The choice is very much up to the individual gardener – how much time do you want to spend thinning out over-enthusiastic wild flowers?

One way in which wild flowers join the border on their own is as 'weeds'. Take a pragmatic approach here, and do not automatically root something out because you did not plant it yourself. If it is a reasonably attractive wild flower that will not spoil your colour scheme or sprawl all over other plants in the border, leave it and see what happens. It may do wonders. Think carefully before you let it seed however, or spread itself too far. A favourite example of mine is herb robert (*Geranium robertianum*), an annual which forms a most attractive mound of pink flowers above finely cut reddish leaves. But if the plant is allowed to seed, there will be hundreds of them coming up next year!

Seasonal considerations

Most borders in today's smaller gardens are what are known as 'mixed borders'; they are composed of a mixture of shrubs, bulbs, herbaceous plants, and sometimes ornamental grasses, annuals and bedding plants too. The idea is that such a blend will provide a succession of interest through the year; spring is the season for shrubs and bulbs, summer for herbaceous plants and annuals, autumn for a few late herbaceous plants and those shrubs that leave the year with a blaze of coloured foliage, while winter is the preserve of evergreens and the herbaceous plants and grasses that have dramatic seedheads. When planning to use wild flowers in a mixed border, you need to consider the seasonal spread of your planting particularly carefully. The chapter entitled Through the seasons

Wild flowers in a small garden

Flowering shrubs and border plants form the framework of this enclosed, south-facing garden, with some wild flowers planted alongside. Cottage garden and cornfield annuals create splashes of colour and a rustic atmosphere. At the back of the garden a trellis screen and an archway bedecked with climbers such as honeysuckle separates off a small wild flower lawn, with an adjacent miniature pond. Tall vegetation, including irises, watermint and meadowsweet, is planted in the wetland area. The shaded border at the base of the far wall is planted with a selection of woodland wild flowers.

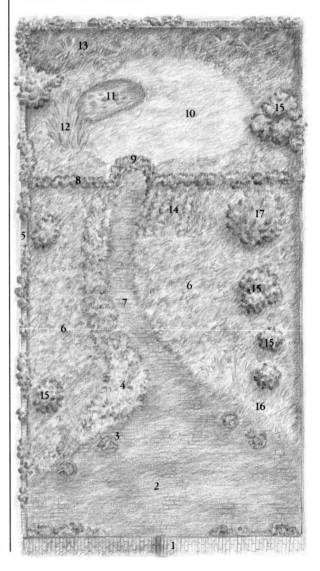

1 *House*
2 *Paved terrace*
3 *Containers planted with wild flowers such as cranesbills*
4 *Planting of cottagey annuals such as Calendula, Limnanthes and Nigella*
5 *Wall clad with climbers such as ivy, clematis, virginia creeper*
6 *Herbaceous border with wild flowers and garden plants: bellflowers, teasels, yarrows and jacob's ladders*
7 *Brick path*
8 *Trellis with honeysuckle, dog roses and climbing roses*
9 *Archway*
10 *Wild flower lawn*
11 *Pond*
12 *Wetland area planted with tall vegetation including irises, watermints and meadowsweets*
13 *Shaded area planted with ferns, sweet cicely, hostas, astilbes, bellflowers and foxgloves*
14 *Vegetable plot planted with salad crops*
15 *Small shrubs*
16 *Cornfield annuals*
17 *Flowering shrub*

(page 103) will give you some ideas on how wild flowers can contribute to the garden at different times of the year.

Herbaceous wild flowers, along with other herbaceous plants, go well with shrubs. Many garden-worthy shrubs are spring- rather than summer-flowering, which can mean that from mid-summer to autumn there is little to look at. This is especially true of those shrubs which follow up spectacular flowering with dull leaves, such as forsythia. However, growing summer wild flowers such as knapweeds (*Centaurea* species) in front of and around spring-flowering shrubs like viburnums, makes the planting look attractive for much longer. You need to ensure that there is adequate spacing (at least 50cm/20in) between newly planted shrubs and wild flowers, otherwise the shrub may not establish properly. But once established, deciduous shrubs can have spring wild flowers such as primroses (*Primula vulgaris*) planted around them and even, if there is space, underneath their branches.

Summer wild flowers that are grown with shrubs in a mixed border need to be in scale. For example some goldenrods (*Solidago* species) can grow to 2m (6½ft), and if they are planted in front of a shrub that is only a metre tall, the shrub will be obscured, while a low-growing hardy cranesbill such as *Geranium sanguineum*, which reaches to only 30cm (1ft), looks insignificant when planted at the foot of a 3m (10ft) high lilac (*Syringa* species). As a general rule, I feel that wild flowers should be between a third and two-thirds of the height of the shrubs they are to accompany in mixed borders.

Most gardens in the temperate zone are at their best in spring and early summer, with a gradual reduction in the number of flowering plants from mid-summer onwards. How to fill the garden with colour during the late summer, often the time when the garden is being used most intensively for recreational purposes, has exercised the minds of many gardeners. There are in fact plenty of admirable wild flowers to choose from for this time of year, many of them North American in origin, their only drawback being that they have a tendency to be tall, perhaps too tall, or a little unkempt, for very small gardens. For many gardeners, bedding plants, such as busy

lizzies (*Impatiens*), petunias and french marigolds (*Tagetes*), are the kingpins of late-summer gardening and I see no reason why they should not be used to make a bright splash of colour among earlier blooming wild flowers.

More appropriate than bedding plants, however, are hardy annuals, which are sown where they are to flower, lasting only one season. Some species will frequently be in bloom long after the main spring and mid-summer wild flower season is over and many have the advantages of being small and easily grown. Among the most colourful species are five-spot baby (*Nemophila maculata*), poached egg flower (*Limnanthes douglasii*) and swan river daisy (*Brachyscome iberidifolia*). There are also those plants that are closely associated with cottage gardens and often thought of as wild flowers in the public imagination: love in a mist (*Nigella damascena*), clary (*Salvia horminum*), pot marigold (*Calendula officinalis*) and cosmos (*Cosmea*).

Grasses are a valuable addition to a garden in autumn, low light through plumed seedheads being especially beautiful. Large, ornamental species can easily be combined with wild flowers and shrubs, although care should be taken that they are not among the minority of very invasive species. The grasses here complement the russet tones of deciduous shrubs in autumn and extend the season of interest for a wild flower planting.

A *wild flower border to attract butterflies*

Wild flowers can be mixed with other border plants or planted on their own in a wild flower border. Here is an example of the sort of border that you can create in a garden, using herbaceous wild flowers rather than conventional border plants. This border will be in full bloom in late summer, often seen as a 'difficult' time for colour in the garden, but a time when butterflies are at their most numerous. The flowers in this selection are all good nectar sources for butterflies and other insects. Most good butterfly plants have masses of small flowers packed together in heads, these being the kind that they find easiest to feed from. Many of these wild flowers also have seedheads in autumn which will be food for small seed-eating birds like finches. All these wild flowers are vigorous, sun loving, easy-going about soil, and can be treated just like any other border plants.

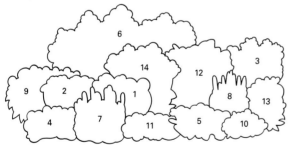

1 *Achillea millefolium* (yarrow): grows to 80cm (32in) with feathery dark green foliage and produces flat heads of white flowers in mid- to late summer; a strong grower.
2 *Asclepias tuberosa* (milkweed): 80cm (32in); one of the best butterfly plants for mid- to late summer.

3 *Aster novae-angliae* (michaelmas daisy, new england aster): to 1.5m (5ft) tall; often flowers into the autumn.
4 *Coreopsis auriculata* (dwarf tickseed): 50cm (20in); a compact habit and a tolerance of some shade make this a useful plant; other coreopsis are larger.

5 *Daucus carota* (wild carrot): to 60cm (2ft); can spread vigorously so be ready to cut it back.
6 *Eupatorium maculatum* (joe pye weed): strong grower, to 2.5m (8ft); does best on damp soil; there are other smaller species as well.
7 *Liatris spicata* (blazing star): grows to 90cm (3ft); an unusual flower shape; looks good

when grown with yellow flowers.

8 *Lobelia cardinalis* (cardinal flower): grows to 90cm (3ft); does best on moist soils.

9 *Monarda didyma* (bergamot, bee balm): grows to 1m (3ft 3in) tall; prefers damp soil.

10 *Origanum vulgare* (marjoram): to 50cm (20in), but often smaller; this wild species is a parent of the culinary herb.

11 *Sedum spectabile* (ice plant): 40cm (16in); often flowers late; avoid the hybrids of this wild flower as they do not attract butterflies.

12 *Solidago odora* (sweet goldenrod): grows to 1.5m (5ft); all the goldenrods are good late-season butterfly plants.

13 *Succisa pratensis* (devil's bit scabious): grows to 90cm (3ft); bushy habit; tolerates some shade.

14 *Verbena bonariensis* (verbena): grows to 1.5m (5ft); long-flowering and unusual; although it may not survive a very cold winter, it will always self-seed.

Several of the best known and most colourful wild flowers were the weeds of traditional cornfields, and these include corn poppy (*Papaver rhoeas*), cornflower (*Centaurea cyanus*) and corncockle (*Agrostemma githago*). These cornfield wild flowers do not have such a long season as many garden annuals, and they need to be sown in succession (see page 84), with sowings made every few weeks in spring and early summer, for a lengthy show. All of these annuals can be grown in odd corners of the garden, wherever there is the smallest area of bare soil, or on a patch that could benefit from brightening up in summer.

Caring for border wild flowers

Wild flowers in borders will often behave differently from the way that they grow in nature or in wild garden settings. Naturally wild flowers tend to grow cheek by jowl, with each other and with grasses. But in a border, without the competition of close neighbours, they have a tendency to grow larger and much more lush. This may be of benefit in a garden but it does also mean that they can grow leggy and lack strength, especially since they no longer have close neighbours to hold them up. Although most wild flowers generally stand up without support and withstand the buffeting of weather and children better than a lot of garden plants, it may sometimes be necessary to provide the kind of support that traditional border plants like delphiniums need.

The hardy cranesbills (*Geranium* species) are a good example of how differently plants grow in the garden. Growing in a meadow or hedgerow, their long flowering stems and long stalked leaves are intermingled with, and supported by, the surrounding grasses and other wild flowers, their flowers poking out among their neighbours over a wide radius. In the garden, grown out of contact with neighbouring plants, the foliage forms neat and attractive hummocks with the flowers at the top, all in a compact mass. After flowering, however, and especially in a wet summer, the plant can collapse, sprawling unattractively over its neighbours.

Wild flowers normally establish quickly in borders, as do most herbaceous plants, getting well into their stride in the second year after planting. Their maintenance needs are not great and they can generally be treated much like any other border plant. As we have seen, there may be a need for thinning out of species that spread vigorously or seed around, and a few species might need staking. But the main task is an annual tidy-up to remove dead stems; this should preferably be done in late winter and early spring, otherwise in the autumn if you live in an area that is not affected by severe winter temperatures. You might also wish to remove dead flowers at regular intervals.

Wild flowers in city gardens

The problems of city gardening are considerable, although there are advantages too. The soil is often thin and full of rubble and the buildings cast heavy shade and funnel the wind in a harmful way to plants. The atmosphere is sometimes polluted. However, one advantage is that towns and cities are always warmer than the surrounding countryside, and the bigger the town the warmer its climate will generally be.

The wild flower gardener, perhaps, faces even more of a challenge than the conventional gardener, since the informality of wild flowers is harder to fit into small gardens. But the key to wild flower gardening in the city is to explore every opportunity and microhabitat. Let climbers romp up anything vertical and small alpine-type wild flowers explore cracks in walls and paving; fill shady nooks and crannies with shade-tolerant ferns and woodlanders; and use containers to soften hard surfaces. With imagination it is amazing how many species can be packed into a small space and how green an urban garden can become.

The role played in town gardens by taller plants, such as shrubs and climbers, is to soften the boundaries or to hide obtrusive buildings. Climbers really come into their own in city gardens, as they fill up a vertical plane without taking up much space on the ground. Consider 'greening' all the walls and fences with climbers such as honeysuckle (*Lonicera sempervirens*), wild pea (*Lathyrus latifolius*) and ivies (*Hedera* species) and erecting trellis for them to climb up, to block unwelcome views from outside. Archways erected over paths provide space for a climber on each

Dodecatheon meadia

Shooting star is a dramatic-looking perennial wild flower that attracts attention in spring; it is so called because, once fertilized, the pale pink flowers turn skywards, their reflexed petals held above the foliage. It is happy in sun or partial shade, provided there is plenty of moisture during its spring growing season. It dies down in summer so drought while the plant is dormant is not a problem. Seed should be sown in the autumn to come up next spring, flowering the year afterwards.

Wild and garden plants have been allowed to colonize every part of this enclosed town garden, climbers scrambling up walls and over the shed as well as softening paving in densely planted containers. Wild flowers used in this way can provide a refreshing element in an urban environment.

SOME WILD FLOWERS SUITABLE FOR THE BORDER

Aquilegia canadensis
This spring-flowering species does well in some shade; it is best grown from seed. Group several plants together for greatest impact.

Gaura lindheimerii
Ideal for trailing through other plants; pure white flowers from mid-summer to autumn.

Myrrhis odorata
An excellent choice for mid-summer flowering (white); attractive ferny foliage and dark brown seedheads. Grows up to 1m/3ft 3in and thrives in semi-shade.

Succisa pratensis
Tough and adaptable, summer-flowering and favoured by butterflies and birds. Grows to 1m/3ft 3in; bushy.

Tanacetum vulgare
Vigorous and tall (up to 1.2m/4ft), best for the back of the border in sun or part-shade. Late flowering, with yellow pompon flowers.

Thermopsis caroliniana
A tough yellow lupin flowering in early summer; attractive foliage and seedheads. Grows to 1.5m/5ft, lasts for years in a sunny border.

side, for example dog rose (*Rosa canina*) and another honeysuckle (*Lonicera periclymenum*), and have the effect of dividing a garden up into 'rooms', enhancing a sense of space.

The challenge of city gardening is to fit as many plants as possible into a small space. An old wall could have plants growing in holes between the stones. Small, limestone-loving wild flowers such as wild pinks (*Dianthus*), wall ferns (*Asplenium* species and *Polypodium vulgare*), stonecrops (*Sedum* species) and numerous alpines will thrive here, often with a minimum of soil. Small wild flowers can grow well in between paving slabs and cracks only a few millimetres wide can support a surprising flora. The wall plants mentioned above will do well, and so will creeping dwarf thymes (*Thymus caespitosus*), deadnettles (*Lamium* species) and chamomile (*Chamaemelum nobile*). The best wild flowers for paving or walls are those that have roots that can follow every crack, throwing forth shoots and flowers metres away from where you planted them. There are several bellflowers that will do this with abandon: *Campanula*

porsharskyana, *C. rotundifolia* and *C. portenschlagiana* as well as alpine toadflax (*Linaria alpina*).

Growing wild flowers in containers will maximize space on areas of paving or in hard-surfaced backyards. A container must have drainage holes in the bottom and a minimum depth of 15cm (6in) is needed for all but the smallest wild flowers; a depth of 30cm (12in) will enable you to grow a good selection. The compost should have enough nutrients to last the whole season: commercially available soil-based potting compost is an ideal medium, provided it is well-drained. Wild flowers grow too vigorously to stay longer than a season in a pot, and you should consider dividing and replanting them every spring. The best wild flowers for container growing are those of medium or small size, with a bushy habit and a shallow rooting system, such as cranesbills (*Geranium* species), euphorbias, bluebells (*Hyacinthoides non-scripta*), knapweeds (*Centaurea*), smaller tickseeds (*Coreopsis* species), scabious (*Scabiosa*, *Succisa* and *Knautia* species), violas and various ferns; the latter must be kept cool and well watered.

Creating wild areas

A garden virtually never has exactly the same conditions in every corner, and the gardener sensitive to the needs of plants can exploit the scope this offers. There may be a slope facing the sun that enjoys a slightly warmer microclimate and sharper drainage, or a tree that casts shade, or a depression where the soil is sometimes waterlogged. Soil conditions can vary surprisingly too, especially in a larger garden, not just because of geological factors but as a result of the operations of developers moving soil around during house construction.

The traditional gardener often sees such conditions as shade or bad drainage as problem areas, but how much better to view them as opportunities, places in which to develop a wilder corner of the garden, growing plants that positively enjoy the prevailing conditions rather than trying to change them. Each variation, however slight, can be used to support a different group of plants. A patch of poor soil in full sun might be the ideal place to start a wild flower meadow; an area of poor drainage could be planted with wetland wild flowers such as the yellow flag iris, loosestrife and cardinal flower, or a shaded area below trees or at the base of a hedge with woodland wild flowers, spring bulbs and ferns.

While the most crucial aspect of planning wild garden features is to place them where the soil and climatic conditions are suitable, there are other considerations too. Some of these are visual – such as how to create a pleasing transition from the tame to the wild within the garden – others practical, such as the question of access and how to incorporate paths and walkways through wilder areas. The most suitable place for a wild area is often considered to be the outer reaches of the garden, which rarely has its full potential realized. Rather than ignore this outer area, or just use it as a backdrop, with more thought it can become part of the garden that you value as much as the rest.

In the following chapter we look at several wild flower 'habitats', or different sets of conditions where a self-supporting group of plants – a plant community – grows. In the wild a particular habitat will generally be found over a wide geographical range, but it is possible to establish plant communities on a much reduced scale within a garden, wherever a certain set of conditions is found. Wild garden habitats can be spectacular on a large scale, as in the completely wild garden (see pages 34–7), but they can also be successfully incorporated as a novel and attractive feature in a medium-sized garden. It is important to understand the wild garden approach, since it involves thinking along quite different lines to traditional gardening methods.

Plant communities

Instead of being planted in the exact places where they are intended to grow, usually in clumps of a single species, the herbaceous plants in a wild garden area are generally grown intermingled, in the way that they would grow naturally, supporting and clambering over each other. Over time, the plants in an established wild garden area form a plant community, a self-supporting group of compatible species. Sharing similar needs for light, moisture and soil conditions, they are able to grow in equilibrium; it is the role of routine operations such as cutting (see page 86), to help maintain this balance. At the same time, a wild garden plant community is dynamic, which means that the equilibrium is maintained by a certain amount of change – plants dying, spreading and moving around. In a meadow planting, for example, some species, such as the annual yellow rattle (*Rhinanthus major*), are short-lived but replace themselves easily by seed. Such a species will move its distribution slightly from year to year.

Competition between plants in a wild garden is greater than in a border, especially in the sun, or in wet environments where plants can grow especially vigorously. In a wild garden it is difficult to give individual attention to plants, because of their number and proximity to each other. To succeed, wild flower species must be suited to the existing conditions of soil and moisture content, light and climate of the wild garden area, otherwise they will be edged out by those that are better adapted.

BELOW *A wild flower feature has been created in this country garden in the form of a drift of meadow beyond the cottage-garden border of roses and delphiniums. It has a good population of ox-eye daisies (Leucanthemum vulgare), which grow vigorously in younger meadows until the grasses establish themselves. Normally a meadow needs to be at least 5 square metres (54 square feet) to contain the beginnings of a representative selection of species.*

ABOVE *A heathland planting is ideal for the soil conditions of this garden, since heather and ling (Erica and Calluna) thrive on acidic soil where many garden plants do not grow well. They form a mesh of tightly packed branches, needing little maintenance apart from an annual or bi-annual clipping. Their flowers are an excellent nectar source for insects.*

What kind of wild area?

To enable you to exploit the different conditions in your garden, we take a look at the main types of wild flower habitat – the plants they support, the growing conditions they need, how long they take to establish, how much maintenance is required thereafter, as well as how to integrate them, and considerations of use and access. In the chapter Establishing wild flower habitats, page 69, you will find the practical information needed to create and maintain the kind of wild garden area best suited to your plot.

Meadows

For the botanist, a meadow is a field of grasses and herbaceous wild flowers that is regularly cut as part of an agricultural process. For the gardener it has

eye daisy (*Leucanthemum vulgare*), self-heal (*Prunella vulgaris*) and meadow buttercup (*Ranunculus acris*). A mix for clay soils (which tend to exacerbate poor drainage) will contain these species and others that do particularly well on clay, such as ragged robin (*Lychnis flos-cuculi*) and betony (*Stachys officinalis*). Many of these species will crop up again in the mix for wet soils, together with a few others that thrive only in moist conditions, such as meadowsweet (*Filipendula ulmaria*) and purple loosestrife (*Lythrum salicaria*). A mix for a chalky soil will include wild flowers that grow well on alkaline soils, like greater knapweed (*Centaurea scabiosa*) and salad burnet (*Sanguisorba minor*). A sandy soil mix will share several species with the chalky one, as both soil types have a tendency to be dry, as well as bird's foot trefoil (*Lotus corniculatus*) and musk mallow (*Malva moschata*).

BELOW *Solomon's seal*
(Polygonatum
multiflorum) *is a
wonderfully elegant
spring-flowering
woodland wild flower.
Unlike many shade-lovers,
it will do fairly well in
drier sites. It spreads
slowly to form a solid
clump after a number
of years.*

ABOVE RIGHT *On a large
scale, this wild flower
meadow forms an
attractive and low-
maintenance garden
feature. Yellow hawkbit*
(Leontodon hispidus) *and
white ox-eye daisy are
intermingled with clover*
(Trifolium pratense). *The
path is mowed frequently.*

come to mean an informal area of grasses and wild flowers that is maintained as an ornamental feature. A true meadow is very much a creature of full sun, and should be placed where it receives direct sunlight for most of the day. Meadows in gardens are usually created by sowing a mixture of wild grasses and wild flower seed, called a meadow mix, and for a garden meadow to be successful the mix needs to be carefully tailored to suit the soil conditions.

Some wild flowers, the most adaptable, will be found in mixes for all soil types and these include ox-

As well as meadow mixes for different soils, suppliers also sell mixes for different seasons, comprising wild flowers that are tolerant of a range of conditions but with an emphasis on flowering at a particular time of year. A spring mix might contain cowslips (*Primula veris*) and meadow buttercup while a summer mix would contain wild flowers like field scabious (*Knautia arvensis*) and wild carrot (*Daucus carota*). In deciding where to put a meadow in a garden, the seasonal aspect needs to be considered. Spring meadows are shorter and are generally kept mown after mid-summer, so they fit more easily into a small garden. Summer meadows are made up of taller wild flowers which look better on a larger scale and, generally, further away from the house. A late summer or autumn meadow, which relies heavily on North American species like goldenrods (*Solidago*) and black-eyed susans (*Rudbeckia*), is even taller.

A meadow is not tidy and ordered, but looks very much as if nature is in control. It is colourful enough to be appreciated by gardeners and visitors when it is in full bloom, but might be criticized for being untidy after the flowers have finished. It is possible to cut it at this stage, but better to leave it, so that the meadow plants can continue to grow and to seed around. Over the winter, when all the top growth is dead, there is still a wild beauty to the seedheads of flowers and grasses waving in the wind, and they are a fine source of food for birds.

A meadow has great potential to be a transitional area between different parts of the garden, for example between lawn and larger shrubs. The soft appearance of meadow is also useful in making boundaries, both visual and real, less jarring and more gradual. From a practical point of view, bear in mind that a summer meadow will be too long to walk through from early summer onwards, so it would usually be better established beyond the more orderly parts of the garden and those areas of grass that are used for recreation. Paths of shorter mown grass can be cut through the meadow to allow access and encourage people to walk through and admire it. In order to prevent wild flowers and grass making inroads into borders or shrub plantings, it is advisable to keep a strip of 1–2 metres (3–6 feet) cut short between them and the taller meadow areas.

Meadows take a good few years to establish. In the second year after sowing, a meadow can certainly look colourful, but it will not be a stable plant community for about five years. During the first few years it will need to be cut regularly to restrict the growth of larger, stronger growing species.

Wild flower lawns

A wild flower lawn is a compromise between a true meadow and a conventional lawn. Unlike the usual lawn though, a variety of wild flowers is encouraged

Wild flowers in a medium-sized garden

The house looks out on to an expanse of wild flower lawn, with a small summer-flowering meadow area beyond. On the right is a herbaceous border containing wild flowers such as bellflowers, cranesbills and knapweeds as well as roses and small shrubs including *Hebe* and *Spiraea*. Behind this are some fruit and other small trees, planted around with shade-loving wild flowers such as primroses and foxgloves as well as ferns, hostas and bugle. A pond with a wetland area imperceptibly joins a border of flowers and shrubs.

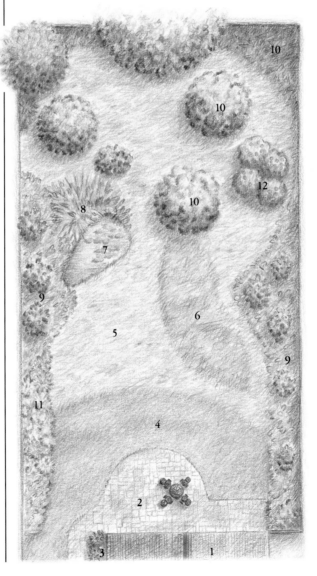

1 *House*
2 *Paved area*
3 *Narrow border along side of house, planted with low-growing perennials such as geraniums and dead-nettles, and shrubs*
4 *Lawn*
5 *Wild flower lawn*
6 *Summer-flowering meadow planted with scabious, meadow cranesbills, yarrows, bedstraws and vetch*
7 *Pond*
8 *Wetland planting, with irises, meadowsweets, astilbes, valerians, marsh marigolds*
9 *Herbaceous planting between roses and shrubs: garden perennials with bellflowers, tansy and small shrubs*
10 *Shady planting in border and under trees: garden perennials (hostas, heucheras, ferns) with bugle, solomon's seals, hellebores, primroses, foxgloves, nettle-leaved bellflowers*
11 *Border planted with cottagey annuals:* Calendula, Nigella *and* Salvia sclarea
12 *Fruit and other small trees*

so that the grass becomes speckled with spots of colour; to many eyes, this is far more attractive than the shaved greensward that is normally seen. It is mown short enough to be used as a lawn is used, for walking across and sitting on, but it will not be suitable for frequently used paths as the flowers would be damaged. Only a lawn seed mix designed for such traffic should be used where this is likely. The most suitable wild flowers for a lawn are late spring to summer flowers, such as daisy, clovers and self-heal. But there are some earlier ones, notably the cowslip and in shadier patches even the primrose if you do not cut the lawn too short.

A wild flower lawn can be grown in an area near to the house and any other part of the garden where short grass is needed for activities or for its appearance. It is the obvious solution for open areas where a full-blown meadow would be too tall or too informal. Strips of wild flower lawn can also act as paths through areas of taller true meadow.

Wild flower lawns are more quickly established than meadows, taking only the same length of time as a conventional lawn until it can be walked on, and about a year for the wild flowers to be mature. It needs to be cut less often than a normal lawn and kept somewhat higher; a surprisingly rich flora can thrive under the blades of a mower.

Areas of shade

Shade in a garden can be caused not only by trees but also by neighbouring buildings or boundary walls, or may simply be on the side of the house that faces away from the sun. Although shady areas are often left uncultivated in gardens, shade can provide a wonderful opportunity to create a small area in which to grow woodland wild flowers.

Spring bulbs can easily be naturalized under trees, which involves planting them in drifts, with the intention that they should slowly spread and need minimal maintainance. Many different kinds of bulb will naturalize easily to give sheets of colour from the last days of winter well into spring. Most of them are adaptable, easy to please plants, needing only good drainage and a reasonably fertile soil. The wild flower gardener will want to concentrate on the original species bulbs rather than the larger number

of cultivars; they have a delicacy and grace about them, yet come in just as wide a range of colours. The most useful species for naturalizing are those that reproduce themselves quickly, each bulb becoming a small clump after a few years: crocuses, snowdrops, daffodils, scillas, leucojums and ornithogalums. Daffodils and narcissi, the classic spring flowers, spread well under deciduous trees; the best species for the wild garden are the wild daffodil (*Narcissus pseudonarcissus*) and the tenby daffodil (*N. obvalaris*), both of which are smaller and more delicate looking than the highly bred daffodils.

Several spring-flowering non-bulbous wild flowers can be naturalized underneath deciduous trees, as they are adapted to make the most of those precious spring days between the end of winter and the sprouting of tree leaves. One of the most startling combinations is that of the pale yellow of primroses with the rich pink of *Cyclamen repandum*; another possibility is to have primroses alongside white wood anemones (*Anemone nemorosa*) and *Anemone blanda*, which flowers in shades of blue, pink and white. These wild flowers are planted as tubers (except for the primrose, which is effectively an evergreen), but they will mainly spread by means of self-seeding.

Many other non-bulbous wild flowers, by nature denizens of the woods, do well in shade, provided it is not too dense. They are rarely as colourful as sun lovers, but they often have a quiet beauty of their own, and most flower early in the year. Low-growing spring wild flowers like violets (*Viola* species), woodruff (*Galium odoratum*) and primroses will be the main source of colour, with the varied foliage of woodland plants such as ferns as the attraction in summer. Other possibilities for autumn interest include the orange berries of lords and ladies (*Arum maculatum* or *A. pictum*) or the red and white berries of doll's eyes (*Actaea* species).

Most shade-loving plants are low-growing, but some are taller, such as solomon's seal, many ferns and hellebores (*Helleborus foetidus*), which can grow to 1 metre (3 feet) tall. This is one of the few woodlanders that seeds itself freely; most spread by stems which root as they go, such as creeping phlox (*Phlox stolonifera*), or by roots that surface to grow new plants, like the woodruff.

Eupatorium purpureum

Joe pye weed is one of the best late-flowering perennial wild flowers and a superb nectar source for bees and butterflies. Being a vigorous, large plant, it is an excellent choice for difficult sites, where there is strong competition from weeds, especially on fertile or moist soils. But who was Joe Pye? The likeliest answer is that this is the corruption of a Native American word meaning typhoid, for which the plant was given as a herbal cure – it was used to induce profuse sweating, which broke the fever. This majestic, upright species has purplish stems which carry heads of pinkish flowers.

The tendency of most shade-loving wild flowers and ferns to grow in a neat shape, coupled with the fact that many are evergreen, makes them admirably suitable for even tiny wild areas within the garden, such as the strip at the base of a fence, an empty corner by a wall, or a bare patch under a single tree. Low-growing evergreen ferns like *Polypodium vulgare* or the christmas fern (*Polystichum acrostichoides*) would be suitable, as well as the silver-splashed leaves of lungwort (*Pulmonaria officinalis*), or the highly scented lily-of-the-valley (*Convallaria majalis*). Since most shade-lovers are spring flowering, you need to consider how attractive the leaves are during the rest of the year; fortunately many of the plants mentioned have interesting foliage too. Several others earn their keep in this respect, including wild gingers (*Asarum* species), with rounded, glossy and sometimes silver-marked leaves, or ivies.

A small woodland wild garden will have to be planted rather than sown. Woodland plants can be slow to establish, especially the less vigorous species that do well in deeper shade, such as trilliums and bloodroots (*Sanguinaria*). If you want quick results, it would be advisable to concentrate on those plants that spread quickly, like periwinkles (*Vinca*) or creeping phlox. As with other habitats, the various woodland plants have different preferences for moist or dry, acid or alkaline soil conditions (see page 54).

Ponds and wetlands

In a conventional garden the pond is likely to be the wildest place: it is the richest habitat for insect and other animal life, and often has a high proportion of native plants. Ponds are the obvious solution for a patch of wet ground – or you may wish to build one on dry land (see page 92). To look at all natural, a pond needs an associated wetland area of lush vegetation, with one side, and preferably more, surrounded by wild flowers of the kind that would naturally grow in the marshy surrounds of a pond.

In a garden it may be undesirable to have wetland planting all the way round; people often want to sit by a pond on dry land, for a start. A wetland area is best placed behind the pond, looking from the main viewpoint, so that its height acts as a background. This relative height could then in turn perhaps be a foreground planting for shrubs and trees behind. If you have the space, one or two small trees or shrubs will give more substance to the planting, especially in winter; willows and alders are ideal. Willows often have attractive foliage, and twigs that glow with warm colours in winter sunlight.

Ponds must be placed in almost full sun, but associated wetland plantings can be in either sun or shade, although the plants in each would be different. The wild flowers of wetlands tend to be big, vigorous growers: joe pye weed, purple loosestrife and yellow flag iris, to say nothing of the majestic grass-like reedmace (*Typha latifolia*) which can grow to 2.5m (8ft) or danubian reed (*Arundo donax*) which can reach 4m (13ft)!

Another way of handling the transition from an open stretch of water to dry land (or dry lawn), is to imitate nature and have a series of progressively drier habitats. An area adjacent to the pond can be kept moist to grow marsh or bog plants in, with an area beyond that is planted with damp-meadow wild flowers, before grading into lawn or meadow. Having a pond in a garden is yet another useful way in which a transition can be made, with tame lawn on one side, perhaps, and wild garden on the other.

In this marshy area water irises (violet Iris versicolor and yellow I. pseudacorus) consort with buttercups (Ranunculus species), ostrich ferns (Matteucia struthiopteris) and candelabra primulas (Primula species). All these plants are more or less equally vigorous and so grow well together.

The totally wild garden

Daffodils (Narcissus) *and crocus form a carpet of colour in spring, providing a natural setting for this house in the country. Species and cultivars of both these plants naturalize easily from bulbs planted in autumn, forming clumps that increase steadily every year. The bulbs could be followed by summer-flowering wild flowers, the meadow being cut in late summer.*

Those lucky enough to have a large country garden will be in a position to create an extensive area of wild garden containing a range of different habitats. Imagine the possibilities offered by wild flower gardening on a large scale: your own meadow, an acre or two of grasses rustling in the breeze; a woodland, with sheets of bluebells and anemones in spring; or a small lake fringed with reeds, irises and other luxuriant waterside vegetation. All wild flower habitats look spectacular on a grand scale, whatever the season. While spring wild flowers, such as primroses and dutchman's breeches (*Dicentra cucullaria*), are attractive in woodlands even on a small and intimate scale, summer-flowering wild flower habitats like meadows, wetlands and heathland are more effective visually on a large canvas, with a myriad of individual flowers creating a mosaic of colour. There is beauty, too, in late autumn and

winter, with the skeletal forms of grass and wild flower seedheads, which look good in snow. Groups of shrubs and small trees such as willows and birches can be attractive in winter, the warm tones of their twigs brought out by low-angled sunlight.

When creating a totally wild garden, it is important to build on what is already there, enhancing any existing habitats, such as meadows and waterside, and taking care to preserve any wild flowers present (see pages 70–1). Any plot with variations in height and aspect will offer different microclimates and these should be fully exploited (see pages 26–31). On a relatively large scale, it is possible to create several different habitats from scratch, by planting trees to make a small woodland area, excavating to develop a pond and wetland, and sowing a variety of different meadow seed mixes (see page 76). Owners of a large garden may be faced with a number of existing trees which are not necessarily native species. But they will provide shelter and shade, at least until the tree species that are part of your plan are mature. The exception might be conifers, especially cypresses whose dense shade makes it difficult to establish anything underneath them.

The habitats you can create will also be influenced by the different types of soil over a given area. As soil can vary even in a small plot, it is worthwhile digging holes to check whether the soil is light, stony and possibly dry, or heavy and potentially waterlogged – and planting accordingly. A poorly drained patch can be used for moisture-loving wild flowers such as ladies' smocks (*Cardamine pratensis*), meadowsweet (*Filipendula ulmaria*) and irises, while a hot, dry bank could become a Mediterranean habitat, supporting drought-resistant shrubs such as cistus and lavender. These different habitats are discussed in greater detail in the next chapter. The pH level of the soil also determines which plants will thrive (see pages 56–7). A bank with a neutral or acidic soil could be planted with heathers and low, shrubby plants such as *Vaccinium myrtillus* and *Gaultheria*, or some attractive grasses such as tufted hair grass (*Deschampsia flexuosa*) and *Molinia caerulea*.

Planting the wild garden

The planting of a totally wild garden should take place in stages; woody plants, including trees, should go in first to form the framework, and herbaceous wild flower planting should be left for a year or two to give the trees and shrubs a headstart. The positioning of plants should be as natural-looking as possible, avoiding sharp boundaries between habitats or clearly delineated clumps of one species. The best way to appreciate how wild plants grow is to look at a stretch of woodland from a good viewpoint, preferably in autumn when it is easier to make out the different tree species. You will notice that the trees are not scattered randomly but have a tendency to group. There may be a cluster of pines in one place, thinning out towards the outside of the group where they become more mixed up with oak and maple. There will then be a stretch where the trees are predominantly oak and maple with the odd pine, possibly a light scattering of pines again, and

then a patch where there is a predominance of maple. The same clustering and fading effect can be seen in meadows but is most obvious when the largest number of species is in flower. This will need to be copied to create naturalistic plantings, particularly at the boundaries between habitats (see pages 40–1).

Time and patience will be needed for the creation of these habitats. Young trees will take decades to become woodland, although many shrubs such as field maple (*Acer campestre*), hazel (*Corylus avellana*) and shadbush (*Amelanchier canadensis*) will have grown to a substantial size after five years. Meadows, however, will look good from the second year onwards, although they will take several more years to settle down into a stable community, with your chosen plants growing strongly and initial weed problems overcome (see pages 72–3). A wetland habitat is the most swiftly established; waterside plants grow rapidly and can make even new lakes look surprisingly mature in the space of a year. Once

A fine spread of squills (Scilla verna) cover the ground in this woodland garden. White wood anemones (Anemone blanda), daffodils and lesser celandine (Ranunculus ficaria) grow in patches, making the most of the spring sunshine. All these species will seed themselves readily.

stable plant communities have been formed, nature can be allowed to take its course. In time, given appropriate maintenance, nature will contribute its own planting schemes and wild flowers that you did not plant will start to appear, making for a richer habitat. As well as supporting different types of flora, a country garden will attract a wealth of fauna. Natures thrives on diversity, and the more habitats you can offer the better, especially if these include areas of water and wetland.

Joining the landscape

A country garden looks best when it joins its surroundings imperceptibly, so that garden and country merge into each other. Even fairly formal country gardens frequently have a 'wilderness area' between the main part of the garden and the surrounding countryside. Wild flowers can do much to manage this subtle transition and so can the planting of locally native trees and shrubs. As the largest elements in any garden, trees have an important psychological effect on one's sense of place. Seen from a distance, the distinction between the garden and the surroundings will be blurred if native trees are planted. Try to avoid on the boundary anything that might look as if it belonged to a more cultivated garden, including bare earth, plants that are obviously not native (like conifers in an area of predominantly deciduous trees), mown grass and rigorously straight lines.

How you handle the garden boundary itself is another crucial factor in blending the garden with the surrounding countryside. The physical boundary at the edge of your property needs to be minimal in character, or at least to look as naturalistic as possible. One solution is to use a 'ha-ha', a sunken wall that was developed by eighteenth-century English landscape gardeners to make boundaries invisible. As the wall is hidden below the line of sight, the distant fields appear to be continuous with the garden. If this is not feasible, try to make boundaries out of local materials. Often the easiest and cheapest way is to plant a hedge, with whatever shrubs are traditionally used in your area. Though a tall hedge will partly block a good view, a mixed country hedge can be used as a feature of the wild flower garden in

Wild flowers for a large country garden

Large expanses of summer meadow with shorter mown paths, surrounded by extensive tree and shrub planting, create an ideal private nature reserve. An area of waterlogged ground at the bottom of a slope is the obvious site for a pond and wetland, planted with tall marshland vegetation, including reeds and reedmace. A steep, dry section of bank has been made into a small heathland planting, with heathers, gorse and broom. An existing hedge on one border has been enhanced with hedgerow wild flowers and climbers such as honeysuckle and wild roses.

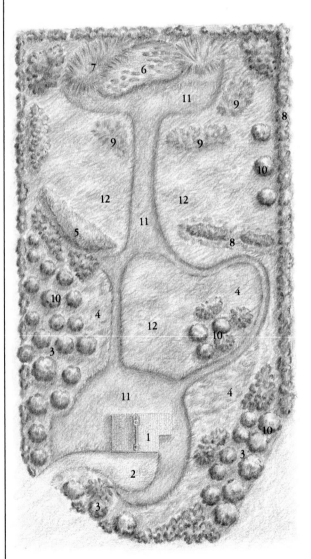

1 *House*
2 *Drive*
3 *Areas of woodland wild flower planting developed under existing and newly planted trees*
4 *Spring meadow, cut short from mid-summer on*
5 *Dry bank, planted with heathers, broom and gorse*
6 *Pond*
7 *Wetland planted with tall marshland vegetation including reeds and reedmace*
8 *Old hedge surrounded by hedgerow wild flowers and climbers (wild roses, honeysuckle)*
9 *Late summer/autumn tall wild flowers: goldenrods, asters, hemp agrimonies*
10 *New trees and shrub plantings*
11 *Wild flower lawn and mown paths cut shorter than surrounding meadow*
12 *Summer-flowering meadow with tall grass and wild flowers*

RIGHT *Tulip cultivars, usually familiar as border plants, can also be grown in a more naturalistic way, scattered across a wild garden meadow area, flowering alongside buttercups. Shorter mown paths, studded with daisies, allow access through the meadow.*

BELOW *Yellow welsh poppies* (Meconopsis cambrica) *and forget-me-nots* (Myosotis alpestris) *are both short-lived perennials but they readily self-sow, as they have done here.*

its own right, and become host to hedgerow wild flowers (see page 60). Hedgerows not only support a great variety of plant and animal life but they are quick to establish, looking surprisingly mature after only a few years.

Think carefully about how you handle the transition on a boundary. Meadows are particularly useful here, and they can be grown wherever there is sunlight for most of the day. Informally planted shrubs and clumps of tall, locally native perennials, such as *Eupatorium* species (hemp agrimony or joe pye weed) or members of the cow parsley family, can be used to create subtle boundaries or to hide fences. Always aim for a random-looking planting, avoiding or concealing straight lines.

Traditional Japanese landscape gardeners have a concept of *shakkei*, which means 'borrowed scenery'. This is not merely a good view, but a view that has been brought into the garden by clever planning, so that distant features are incorporated as part of the backdrop. Wild flower planting in the foreground of such a view will help to integrate the scenery beyond by bringing a bit of nature into your garden.

Designing wild flower plantings

A variety of wild flowers is displayed in this North American spring woodland. Sheets of creeping phlox (Phlox stolonifera) *cover the ground, and in the foreground are the white spikes of foam flowers* (Tiarella cordifolia), *red columbines* (Aquilegia canadensis) *and the fronds of the evergreen christmas fern* (Polystichum acrostichoides).

The forms that plants take are many: trees, shrubs, climbers, herbaceous perennials, bulbs and annuals. While we are mainly concerned here with the herbaceous perennials that people understand as 'wild flowers', a garden, like the majority of natural plant communities, is composed of woody plants, bulbs, climbers, grasses and annuals too. We need to consider how the wild flower gardener is to combine several different kinds of plant in a garden, to create the kind of environment that he or she wants. Interest and beauty at all times of year is important for most of us, and the provision of habitats and feeding grounds for wildlife is a factor that the wild flower gardener will probably be interested in too. The way that different forms of plant are combined can influence how effectively the garden fulfils the roles that are expected of it.

The framework

The framework of a garden is generally provided by trees and larger shrubs, and the wild flower garden is no exception. Within this framework, most of the planting of a wild flower garden will involve herbaceous plants, bulbs, ferns, grasses and, to some extent, smaller shrubby plants.

Trees

Trees are very much the backbone of a garden: they can frame views, they can hide eyesores, they can shut a garden off from the outside world or simply act as a backdrop. They also influence the environment in a garden by casting shade and breaking the force of the wind. All these factors, together with the time it takes a tree to mature, and its relative permanency, make the planting of a tree a matter for careful consideration.

There are many arguments in favour of planting a majority of native trees. Most important of all, the species native to your area, and preferably propagated from stock obtained locally, will be the best adapted to the prevailing conditions. They will be accustomed to the extremes of temperature and the levels of rainfall that your area receives. Native trees also visually fit better into the local landscape. The sight of some introduced trees can spoil a distinctive local view; for example, the introduction of cypresses and eucalyptus into a traditional agricultural landscape of fields, hedges and deciduous trees can be very intrusive. Native trees can be of far more use to local wildlife too, especially specialized insect species.

When planning to introduce trees you need to be well aware of how big they are going to grow and their effect on the rest of the garden. Give careful thought to what you might want to grow underneath since the influence different kinds of tree have on what will grow under them varies considerably. Many evergreens cast such dark shade that virtually nothing will grow below them. Pines, although they often cast a light shade, produce acidic leaf litter which does not suit all plants. Some deciduous trees, notably beeches (*Fagus* species) and maples (*Acer* species), and especially the European sycamore (*Acer pseudoplatanus*), not only cast a dense shade, but so effectively suck moisture and nutrients out of the soil around them that very few wild flowers will grow underneath. If you want only light shade, then birches (*Betula* species) are undoubtedly one of the best trees, as they are fast-growing, adaptable and compatible with a wide range of wild flowers.

Shrubs

The importance of shrubs in the layout of a garden lies in their ability to provide height and fill space all year round, in contrast to herbaceous plants that die back during the winter. When planning a garden, make sure you know how big the shrubs are going to get, and leave plenty of space for wild flowers among and in front of them. Shrubs can be effectively used to divide up the garden and thus help to create a distinct atmosphere in different parts of it. Shrubs are also important in providing nesting and roosting places for birds, and are best grown in clumps for this purpose. Many shrubs, such as *Viburnum*, *Cotoneaster* and *Prunus*, have berries that can play a vital role in feeding birds like thrushes and finches throughout the winter.

It has to be said that many gardens, especially small ones, are overplanted with shrubs, and that since many of the most popular, such as forsythia and many viburnums, are early flowering, they provide no colour after mid-summer. Combining them with late blooming wild flowers, such as michaelmas daisies (*Aster* species) and *Eupatorium* species (hemp agrimony and joe pye weed), is a way of lengthening the season of interest.

Whether or not to plant shrubs that are native to your area is not such a crucial question as it is with trees, their impact on the landscape being less. I favour the planting of a balance of attractive native species with introduced ones, selected both for their worth as garden plants and their compatibility with the natives and with wild flowers. A good example of an introduced but garden-worthy shrub might be the shadbush (*Amelanchier*), a large shrub or small tree with attractive early flowers, bright autumn colour and a plentiful supply of fruit for the birds. Its quiet beauty is appropriate to gardens far beyond its North American home.

Many shrubs and small trees have berries that are not only pleasing to us, but offer an important food source for birds in winter. Certain berry-bearing species, such as *Juniperus virginiana*, are notable in that they are not touched until later in the winter, which means that they are a particularly crucial food supply. Woody plants that bear nuts, for example *Corylus avellana*, are also an important food source for birds and for mammals like squirrels.

Sub-shrubs

Smaller woody plants are a distinctive feature of many plant communities, for example, ling and

Cowslips (Primula veris) and bluebells (Hyacinthoides non-scripta) grow among grasses in a meadow area at the edge of a large country garden. The ha-ha beyond acts as a natural-looking boundary, allowing the landscape beyond to be continuous with the garden.

heather (*Calluna vulgaris* and *Erica* species) and bilberry (*Vaccinium myrtillus*) on windswept moorland, or cistus and lavender on dry Mediterranean hillsides. These are obviously the wild plants to concentrate on when you garden in the kind of harsh environment where these plants grow naturally, but they also have their uses in other places. A hot, dry bank with shallow soil might be more successful planted with cistus, albeit far from its home territory, than with local wild flowers. Low evergreen shrubs like heathers and brooms (*Cytisus* species) can also be used in borders among wild flowers and cultivated border plants to provide some colour and form in the winter.

Climbers

Climbers have an important role to play in the garden, particularly in softening hard surfaces such as fences and walls, and can do much to give small city gardens a more rustic feel. They provide shelter and feeding grounds for insects and birds. Climbers can also be trained up established trees and will send forth their flowers from among the branches. This effect can even be achieved on dead trees, so avoiding their expensive and often hazardous removal – in many a country garden, a wild rose or honeysuckle has taken over and beautified a tree that would otherwise have had to be felled.

There are always plenty of climbers in a country hedgerow, romping along horizontally as well as vertically, their leaves, flowers and berries adding to the rich, visual appeal of an established hedge. Summer-flowering wild roses, clematis and honeysuckle provide colour after the main season of spring wild flowers is over, while other hedgerow plants, such as virginia creepers (*Parthenocissus* species), and vines (*Vitis* species) provide good autumn colour. Ivy is a particularly useful climber as it is one of the few evergreen species and does not harm trees. A word of warning: certain climbers such as old man's beard (*Clematis vitalba*) and japanese honeysuckle (*Lonicera japonica*), are very vigorous and so careful selection of species is important, especially in small gardens.

Very few climbers can support themselves, except virginia creepers and ivy that can attach themselves to more or less any surface. Those climbers that grow by twining or using tendrils, such as vines, will need to be supplied with trellis or wire to cling to if they are to be grown against a wall or fence.

Herbaceous wild flowers

These plants that die down to ground level every winter, are the ones that the wild flower gardener will be most interested in growing. Their advantages are that they are, for the most part, quick growing and easy to establish, their disadvantages that they are usually of minimal interest in winter, and that the majority of larger species flower only from late spring onwards. A garden composed entirely of herbaceous plants can seem formless; shrubs are needed to provide structure and to furnish some colour early in the year. Yet for most of the growing season they are unrivalled as a source of colour and interest. Those wild flower habitats important for the majority of gardeners – meadows, wetlands and woodland – owe nearly all their interest to herbaceous plants in one form or another.

Grasses

Most gardens have some grass, and yet the ornamental qualities of grasses as a group of plants are seriously underestimated. A wild flower lawn or meadow consists mostly of grasses, but they are usually seen only as a backdrop for the more colourful flowers. Yet some grasses are very beautiful in their own right, and they deserve to be given a much higher profile in the garden. With their close relatives the sedges and rushes, grasses are perhaps best appreciated in autumn and winter, when their brown and yellow seedheads, in a variety of shapes, are seen waving in the breeze.

Some regions have a rich variety of large and dramatic grasses: bluestems (*Andropogon*) and switch grass (*Panicum virgatum*) from North America can be used in borders alongside late flowering perennials and shrubs, and they look magnificent through the winter. The European species are smaller and less dramatic, but there are some underrated beauties: the fine pink haze of a meadow of yorkshire fog (*Holcus lanatus*), the delicate panicles of tufted hair grass (*Deschampsia flexuosa*) or the distinctive flowerheads of wood melick (*Melica uniflora*). These smaller

SHRUBS AND SMALL
TREES FOR WILDLIFE
Amelanchier
A group of large shrubs from North America, with white flowers in spring, purple berries and orange leaves in autumn.
Betula
Hardy and adaptable, ideal for small gardens, most species have silver bark; birch seed is a rich food source for wildlife.
Cornus
North American species are spectacular, with masses of white or pink flowers in spring and berries in autumn.
Ilex
Invaluable to the gardener for their evergreen leaves, and to birds for berries.
Prunus
The pink or white flowers are renowned as harbingers of spring. Nearly all species have fruit which is attractive to birds.
Sorbus
Fine all-round small trees: all species have white flowers in spring, followed by berries and good autumn colour.
Viburnum
Viburnums offer us spring or winter flowers and the species will provide autumn fruit. The winter-flowering species are rewarding garden shrubs.

grasses are best appreciated en masse, in a meadow or lightly shaded woodland area. Grass seedheads of any kind are valuable for feeding small birds like finches and thrushes as well as small mammals.

Bulbs

Bulbs provide early spring flower at a time when the majority of herbaceous plants are still dormant. In a small garden, with little room for spring shrubs, they are especially appreciated. In many gardens, wild bulb species like the wild daffodils (*Narcissus pseudonarcissus*) and crocuses will be the main source of colour until late spring. Even after that, when the main focus of interest has shifted onto herbaceous species, there are bulbs worth considering, such as camassias (*Camassia esculenta*), whose blue starry flowers in early summer are especially useful on damp ground, and of course the lilies, some of which, like the martagon lily (*Lilium martagon*), can

This small hedgerow planting makes part of an attractive boundary between a garden and the field beyond. Lupins (Lupinus *species) and ox-eye daisy* (Leucanthemum vulgare) *grow alongside red campion* (Silene dioica). *Red campion is one of the finest early summer wild flowers, being colourful and easy to establish, doing best on slightly damp soils.*

be naturalized in meadows or, such as the turk's cap lily (*L. superbum*), in woodland. At the other end of the year there are various bulbs that send up flowers in autumn, leaving the foliage to emerge in spring, such as autumn crocus (*Colchicum* species). The foliage that some bulbs, notably narcissus, leave behind after they have flowered is often regarded as untidy by gardeners. But in wild flower gardening it can be effectively concealed with grass and later flowering herbaceous species.

Bluebells (Hyacinthoides non-scripta) *are one of the finest wild flower spectacles; they are also quite easy to establish. Once the bulbs have been planted, they self-sow to form dense colonies in lightly shaded areas.*

Annuals

Annual plants complete their life cycle germinating, flowering and seeding in one year. In temperate climates they do not play a major role in plant communities, unable to survive the competition from larger perennial species, but in drier climates they can be a prominent part of the local flora. However, agriculture and other human activities such as road-building, by constantly disturbing the soil, have given some annual species a toehold in climates where they would otherwise be rare or even non-existent; examples include mainly cornfield flowers like poppy (*Papaver rhoeas*) and cornflower (*Centaurea cyanus*).

Only in seasonally dry climates can annuals be regarded, or even maintained, as a major part of a natural plant community, but they are so cheerfully colourful, quick growing and easy to establish, that they have earned themselves a place in the wild flower gardens of many moist climates. A small patch of cornfield annuals, often refreshed with new seed every year, can be one of the brightest parts of a garden. In drier climates annuals such as california bluebells (*Nemophila menziesii*), linanthus (*Linanthus grandiflorus*) and purple heliotrope (*Phacelia tanacetifolia*) can play a key part in the wild flower garden.

Planting effects

In a wild garden, or a small wild area, we like to be convinced that what we see is natural, or could be. The art of planting a wild garden is to make it seem as if everything has arrived there by natural agency, from the wind blowing in seeds to squirrels burying nuts. A key to naturalistic planting is always to avoid hard edges, sudden boundaries and straight lines. The best way to learn how to plant 'naturally' is to look at the way nature plants, at how wild flowers distribute themselves around meadows, and how shrubs and trees sometimes scatter, sometimes cluster themselves across woodland. In nature you will be unlikely to come across an area that is composed entirely of one species. Plants generally grow in communities, often made up of a surprising number of species, in which the individuals grow together in an intricate mix, twining round each other.

Planting in drifts

Wild plants do not grow at random. Their scattering and clustering effect is often the result of different environmental factors, such as areas of greater soil moisture. Sometimes it is even possible to identify areas of wet ground from afar in this way, just as the creamy drifts of meadowsweet (*Filipendula ulmaria*) mark out the areas of damp ground in many European meadows. The meadowsweet in the damp part of the field does not end suddenly – the plant gradually thins out before disappearing entirely, perhaps being progressively replaced with another wild flower more tolerant of dry conditions.

When planting wild flowers, or sowing seed, try to imitate this drifting effect. Plant one species thickly in the middle of the drift and progressively thin it out towards the outside; let your drifts interpenetrate, blend, swirl into and out of each other. Think about how this will work from a distance too. Narrow drifts of wild flowers, planted at right angles to the main viewpoint, are particularly effective because the eye travels over a succession of different flower colours or leaf forms. Taller planting, such as clumps of shrubs or larger wild flowers, can be planted among shorter grasses and

wild flowers, thus creating rivers of flowing space.

In time the plants themselves will rearrange things; some species will do better in one area than another and will displace each other accordingly. Over the years, as seeds are scattered and grow, and older plants clump up or thin out, the planting will increasingly take on a life of its own. Most exciting of all are the possibilities of other wild flowers seeding in from outside, gifts of the wind and of wildlife. In the country this can happen quickly, and the enrichment of your creation by nature is one of the greatest rewards of wild flower gardening.

Plant and colour combinations

Getting the colour associations right can be quite a challenge in the conventional garden. You may be exercised about whether to dare to put that purple next to this red, how to lighten the colours in this corner. In the traditional border, plants are grown in clumps, which intensifies the colours but means that the gardener has to think carefully which colours can be juxtaposed. The wild flower gardener, by comparison, has an easier time since wild flowers grow in a scattered, more random way. Have you ever seen a badly colour-schemed meadow or a garish spread of woodland flowers? The reason you have not is that the individual flowers are all mixed together, with grasses and leaves whose greens and browns act as a 'visual buffer' between colours that might clash.

This is not to say that the wild flower gardener can disregard colour scheming altogether. Colours can be mixed haphazardly on a large scale and not much will go wrong, but on a smaller scale care needs to be taken. In a small garden, or in a more formal feature such as a wild flower border, you need to consider how the colours will work with their surroundings. In a confined space it is best that the range of colours is somewhat restricted. Choose one or two colours that go together well and draw up a list of plants suitable for the site which have flowers in shades of these colours. An example would be to choose blue and pink, and to have primarily meadow cranesbills with pink musk mallow, two meadow species that

Primula veris

An extremely popular European wild flower, in some areas the cowslip was almost picked to extinction but it has now made a comeback and it spreads readily, especially on chalk soils. One of the finest and most delicate of country wines was once made from cowslip flowers, and cowslip-flower syrup was used as a cough remedy. This clump-forming perennial is associated with St Peter, as the nodding flowers reminded people of a bunch of keys, which the saint holds in his role as gatekeeper of heaven.

complement each other beautifully. They could be joined by meadow scabious, with its lavender blue flowers or some of the pink-flowered cranesbills.

Since one of the characteristics of wild flower gardening is the buffering effect of foliage on flower colours, think about what grasses, ferns and other foliage plants will look good with what flowers. For example, grasses with a bluish sheen such as the American bluestems (*Andropogon*) are a good match for pink, mauve and purple flowers like those of bergamot (*Monarda didyma*) and ironweed (*Vernonia*). Wild flowers with attractive evergreen foliage are always valuable, especially in winter, like the hellebores and shade-tolerant ferns. Several shade-loving ground covers have attractive evergreen leaves too.

Be bold and experiment. Most of this book is about how to create plant communities based on what grows together naturally and locally. But there are adventurous gardeners around who are creating landscapes with ornamental grasses and wild flowers selected from all over the world, and grown together because they make a simply stunning combination.

ABOVE *Restricting wild flower plantings to a few colours that work well together can create some beautiful effects. Steely-blue* Eryngium planum *and pinky-red* Knautia macedonica *look stunning together. Effective colour combinations often occur when chance brings two plants into juxtaposition.*

LEFT *Wild flowers look most natural grown in drifts, as in this intermingling of orange Californian poppy* (Eschscholzia californica) *and baby blue eyes* (Nemophila menziesii).

A LOOK AT WILD FLOWER HABITATS

A habitat is a home, somewhere that offers the right conditions for a flower species to grow well, and to compete successfully with its neighbours for light, water and space. Wild flowers generally grow together in plant communities, each habitat being a natural home for a different community. In this chapter we look at meadows, woodlands, wetlands and dry heathlands, through a gardener's eyes, seeing why particular plants grow where they do. These habitats and the communities of wild flowers they support can be used as an inspiration and guide for creating your own wild garden areas.

The rich colouring of the wild flowers blowing in the wind in this mountain meadow serve to remind us that wild flowers can be as colourful as garden plants. The pink is greater knapweed (Centaurea scabiosa), *the white is yarrow* (Achillea millefolium), *both of which thrive on limestone soils, and stay colourful later in the summer than many other species. Both are first-rate wild flowers for the garden.*

Meadows

This early summer scene at the edge of a meadow shows a number of colourful and vigorous wild flowers: the lacy white heads of sheep's parsley (Anthriscus sylvestris), yellow meadow buttercups (Ranunculus acris) and lilac wood cranesbill (Geranium sylvaticum). These wild flowers are a particular feature of fertile soils.

When we think of wild flowers most of us think of meadows, acres of grass rippling in the breeze, a myriad dots of colour on a background of green and golden brown. If we want to grow wild flowers ourselves, it is often this colour-spattered effect that we wish to create. But first we need to look at meadows and understand what they are – and the most important fact to know is that meadows are hardly ever natural. The prairies of North America and the steppes of eastern Europe are natural, but elsewhere meadow habitats are the result of human activity and exist as part of an agricultural process.

A meadow is for cutting – its function is to produce hay to feed farm animals in winter; any other characteristic it has, such as being full of beautiful flowers, is entirely secondary! Some meadows are left as they are for years, being cut once or twice annually, some are grazed by cows, sheep or horses from time to time, and others are ploughed up by the farmer and re-sown every few years.

The traditional meadow is an ideal habitat for a wide range of sun-loving herbaceous plants. Woody plants, which cannot continue if cut down every year, are prevented from growing, allowing smaller plants, which shoot up from the base each year, to thrive. Constant cutting can control the growth of the more vigorous grasses and wild flowers as well, giving slow-growing species an opportunity to establish themselves. If the farmer were to leave the land alone, however, shrubs and trees would start to grow and in a few years the meadow would disappear beneath thick scrub vegetation.

When the agricultural process changes, so does the meadow and this is why meadows are so much poorer in wild flowers today. One of the major changes in agriculture in this century has been the introduction of nitrogen-rich fertilizers to stimulate fast growth and therefore give greater yields of grass for feeding cattle. The plants that can utilize the nitrogen best and grow the quickest then begin to

RIGHT *Poppies (Papaver rhoeas) are one of the brightest wild flowers, but live for just one year and will only form a mass of colour like this on soils that are regularly disturbed by ploughing. They are joined by corn chamomile (Anthemis arvensis) and a vetch (Vicia), two other annual species. If this field were left undisturbed, the grasses and other perennial wild flowers, will establish a thick turf that will gradually exclude the poppies and other annual species that need to re-seed every year in order to survive.*

force out slower-growing species such as many wild flowers. This process is exacerbated by another modern practice, that of using specially bred fast-growing grasses, notably rye grasses. These grow so vigorously that nothing else stands a chance. Indeed, a modern farm can easily contain fewer species of plant than a stretch of desert! Many of the wild flowers seen in the meadows of our ancestors' day have disappeared because they have simply lost the battle for survival with nitrogen-fed rye grass.

Different soils have their own distinct kinds of meadow. The flowers and grasses that grow well on wet soils tend not to do well on dry soils, and vice versa. On poorly drained soil you will find wetland flowers like loosestrife (*Lythrum* and *Lysimachia* species), globe flower (*Trollius* species), lady's smock (*Cardamine pratensis*), ragged robin (*Lychnis floscuculi*) and meadowsweet (*Filipendula ulmaria*) that thrive in such conditions. There is another range of wild flowers that do well in soil that is light and holds little moisture; these include the knapweeds (*Centaurea* species), scabious (*Scabiosa* and *Knautia* species) and mallows (*Malva* species). On thin chalk or limestone soil you will find one of the most beautiful and interesting of all grassland floras, that of the chalkland meadow (see page 49), including the pasque flower (*Pulsatilla vulgaris*), restharrow (*Ononis repens*) and harebell (*Campanula rotundifolia*). Even the richest wild flower meadow is still a battleground for survival, as competition between species is intense and the frequency or timing of cutting can have a dramatic effect on the balance of species (see page 86).

We can still try to re-create the meadows of the past, but making a good meadow takes effort and at least several years (see pages 76–9). It is best to grow a mixture of species appropriate to your soil and site, as working with nature will always give better results. If you are starting your meadow with a ready-made, commercially available grass and wild flower seed mixture (see page 76), you should be able to choose from a range of mixtures that are blended for specific different soils.

Seasonal meadows

Since meadows have come into existence through a balance of forces between humans and nature, the type of plant community that flourishes will depend on the agricultural practices being followed. Traditional European meadows, where the hay is cut after mid-summer, have wild flowers that are at their most colourful between late spring and cutting; on the whole these are tall species, like knapweed and meadow cranesbill (*Geranium pratense*), or scramblers like common vetch (*Vicia sativa*) that climb up their companions to pull themselves into the light. Such a meadow will have some colour earlier in the year, with ragged robin in damper spots for instance, or cowslips (*Primula veris*) in drier. Pastures, which are grazed for months at a time by cattle, cannot develop the flora of tall wild flowers that are characteristic of summer hay meadows, but may often have colourful spring flowers, especially those like buttercup (*Ranunculus* species), which is poisonous and recognized as such by grazing animals. The gardener can manipulate a wild flower meadow at home to encourage a predominance of either spring or summer species: cutting late will allow tall, summer-flowering ones to dominate; cutting earlier in the season, and more frequently, will give shorter, spring-flowering species a better chance.

Spring meadows

Bulbs tend to be predominant among early spring wild flowers, as their reserves of stored food give them a headstart. There are many different kinds that naturalize readily in grass, each bulb becoming a small clump after a few years, such as crocuses, wild tulips (*Tulipa sylvestris*) and daffodils. They give sheets of colour from the last days of winter well into the spring. Growing bulbs in naturalized drifts is quite common gardening practice, but to create impact in a wild garden setting a great number are needed. Consequently the most useful species are those that reproduce themselves quickly.

The common snowdrops (*Galanthus nivalis*) and the golden-flowered aconites (*Eranthis hyemalis*) appear during the last days of winter; they thrive in short grass in some shade, where they form good-sized clumps after a few years. A little later, crocuses can be found growing in well drained meadows in sunny sites, where the grass is not cut until mid- or late spring. *Crocus tommasinianus*, with violet flowers, is one of the most vigorous species.

Daffodils and narcissi, the classic spring flowers, spread well in grass in both sun and light shade. The graceful proportions and natural style of the wild species are seen in the small wild daffodil (*Narcissus pseudonarcissus*), the tenby daffodil (*N. obvalaris*) and the poet's narcissus (*N. poeticus*). Primroses (*Primula vulgaris*) and oxlips (*P. elatior*) will also thrive along meadow edges, where they receive some shade from trees, or on shaded slopes.

Bluebells and fritillaries are best known as plants of open woodland, but they can be seen growing in wild flower meadows that are not cut until early summer, nor are too full of larger wild flowers. In grass, they do not form the sheets of shimmering blue that you will find in the woods, but few other meadow flowers are such a clear blue. The mysteriously named snake's-head fritillary (*Fritillaria meleagris*) is one of the finest late-spring flowers of Europe, although now rare in the wild; it is most likely to be found in a damp, not waterlogged, sunny meadow.

The first non-bulbous flowers tend to start at the same time as the daffodils. The dead nettles grow well on any soil, in sun or shade. They have invasive tendencies, but as meadow plants they are kept in check by the grasses. One of the classic European spring wild flowers, the cowslip, was once very common, but is now reduced in numbers. However, it is good to see its sheets of yellow making a comeback on motorway cuttings. It grows in quite short grass, preferably in dry conditions, provided the grass is not cut during its growing season; if allowed to seed, it spreads prolifically. Other familiar spring wild flowers that will flourish in garden meadows include buttercup and, in damper spots, lady's smocks (*Cardamine pratensis*).

Summer meadows

This is the wild flower habitat we all really want; the very words conjure up romantic dreams of lazing away hot days in the countryside, surrounded by gently rustling grass and flowers. The 'flowery mead'

RIGHT *Wild daffodils (Narcissus pseudonarcissus) are a lovely springtime feature of old pastures and meadows in European hilly regions, where little nitrogen-rich fertilizer is used, allowing a wide variety of wild flowers to thrive.*

LEFT *The unimproved summer meadow is a wonderfully rich habitat, capable of containing an enormous number of wild flower species. In early summer red clover* (Trifolium pratensis), *red campion* (Silene dioica) *and meadow buttercups* (Ranunculus acris) *flower together. These wild flowers are among those that cope better than many with modern agricultural practices, and are easy to establish in a wild garden.*

47

After mid-summer the white heads of yarrow (Achillea millefolium) are a distinctive feature of meadows and other open habitats. It grows here alongside the bright yellow corn marigold (Chrysanthemum segetum) and blue cornflower (Centaurea cyanus), both annuals, which shows that this area must have been disturbed, by ploughing for example, within the last few years.

praised by medieval writers was one of the earliest recorded appreciations of the beauty of wild flowers.

In mid-summer the majority of meadow wild flowers are in bloom, producing a sea of colour. The daisy family gets into its stride, as well as vigorous flowers such as knapweeds, yarrow and meadow cranesbill in Europe, and sunflowers (*Helianthus angustifolius*), coreopsis and coneflower (*Echinacea* species) in North America. Another important group is the pea family (Leguminosae); this includes clovers (*Trifolium* and *Lespedeza*), wild pea (*Lathyrus*), lupins (*Lupinus perennis*), vetches (*Vicia*) and tick trefoils (*Desmodium*). Some stand tall, like the tick trefoils and bush clovers, while others, such as the vetches, are climbers. All pea flowers play an important part in the life-cycle of meadows. They have nodules on their roots, inhabited by bacteria which turn atmospheric nitrogen into nitrates, the only form in which plants can absorb this crucial element. When a pea flower root or stem dies and decays, the nitrogen is available for other plants to use.

Late summer/autumn meadows

By late summer, European meadows and roadsides display only the occasional patch of colour, with yarrow, scabious (*Scabiosa* and *Succisa*) and thistles. Eastern North America on the other hand has a huge range of late-blooming wild flowers, a few of which, such as phlox and michaelmas daisy (*Aster*), have made their way into garden borders worldwide. Most are large-growing members of the daisy family (Compositae), although many might not be immediately recognizable as such. Tall and majestic, if a little untamed in appearance, these late wild flowers are immensely colourful. Yellow is dominant, as seen in the numerous species of goldenrod (*Solidago*) and the daisies of black-eyed susans (*Rudbeckia*) and sunflowers (*Helianthus* species). But there are also the purples and violets of michaelmas daisies, the distinct pink-shot violet that is special to ironweed (*Vernonia*), the pinks of bergamots (*Monarda*) and the subtly coloured hazy flowers of joe pye weeds (*Eupatorium* species). They are all excellent butterfly plants too.

*The thin, but rich, vegetation in this piece of meadow is typical of chalk downland: there are wild flowers like pyramidal orchid (*Anacampsis pyramidalis*), and bird's foot trefoil (*Lotus corniculatus*) (bottom right corner) which cannot compete with larger growing, more vigorous species. It is also interesting to see ox-eye daisy (*Leucanthemum vulgare*) which grows rampantly on fertile soils, but forms a much smaller plant on thin chalk soil.*

Chalk meadows

The chalk downland habitat, found on limestone hills in northern Europe, supports a rich community of plants, many of them very beautiful. In nature a chalk downland flora depends on the close grazing of sheep and rabbits to maintain a low and tight sward, and it is particularly vulnerable to changing land use. The grasses and wild flowers of these places can cope with the dry, stony soils that defeat plants from lusher terrain. Many of them are plants that would be easily smothered by larger vegetation, which has happened in areas where grazing has been significantly reduced or fertilizers used.

Some chalk-loving wild flowers are small, verging on what might be loosely described as alpine, such as wild thyme, cheddar pink (*Dianthus gratianopolitanus*) and the harebell (*Campanula rotundifolia*). Several are slow, methodical growers, used to living on a poor, thin soil. One of the earliest is the pasque flower (*Pulsatilla vulgaris*), whose sumptuous purple

flowers emerge from a ruff of silky-haired leaves with remarkable rapidity. A feature of many chalk-meadow flowers is their clear blue – quite a rare flower colour but most frequently found among dwellers on chalk and limestone. The blues of the European gentians can have a stunning intensity. The spring gentian (*Gentiana verna*) sets enormous quantities of seed, which means it can spread well. The most spectacular flowers of chalk meadows are the numerous species of orchid such as the bee orchid (*Ophrys apifera*) and the pyramidal orchid.

You do not need to have chalk soil to establish a downland flora in your garden. A pile of builder's rubble could even be successfully transformed by covering it with a thin layer of garden soil, then planting it up to make an artificial chalk bank. If the soil is really thin, only the smallest species will survive. Weeding is the most important aspect of maintenance since many of the plants are not strong growers. Weeds should be removed individually and the area cut to 5cm (2in) regularly (see page 86).

A cornfield wild flower meadow like this is spectacularly colourful, although short-lived. *Poppies* (Papaver rhoeas), *cornflowers* (Centaurea cyanus) *and corn chamomile* (Anthemis arvensis), *all originally weeds of cornfields, flower for around a month in summer, although in the garden sowings can be made at different times to extend the season.*

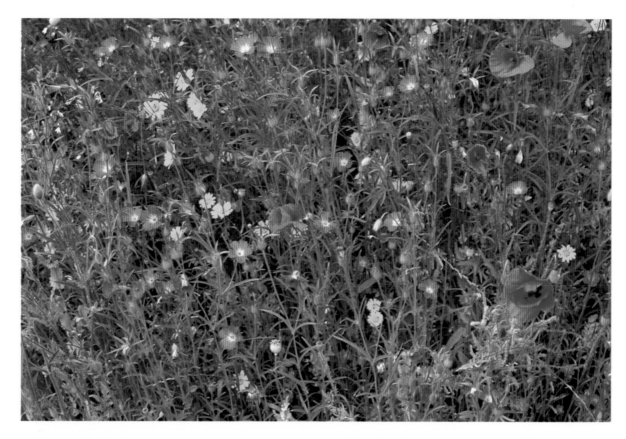

The mauve corncockle (Agrostemma githago) flowers alongside poppies and corn chamomile. Once reviled as a weed whose toxic seeds poisoned the harvest, it is now rare as a wild flower in an agricultural setting, but makes an easy annual in the garden, flowering a few months after sowing.

Cornfields and annual meadows

One of the most dramatic wild flower spectacles is that of an old-fashioned cornfield splashed with the fierce red of poppies (*Papaver rhoeas*), along with a spattering of blue and mauve cornflowers (*Centaurea cyanus*), mauve corncockles (*Agrostemma githago*) and the brilliant yellow of corn marigolds (*Chrysanthemum segetum*). 'Old-fashioned' is the right word because this is a rare sight nowadays. The cornfield wild flowers of today were the 'pernicious weeds' of the past, which grew every year because it was impossible to clean cereal seed adequately. Modern seed is clean and any surviving flowers can be sprayed with herbicide, so many of the cornfield weeds of Europe are now quite rare, although the red poppy survives. Its dormant seed will last for decades, so whenever the embers of its old habitats are disturbed, by road building for instance, it flares into life again.

Cornfield flowers are annuals of disturbed soils, quick-growing opportunists that fill vacant ground until other slower-growing but perennial grasses and flowers establish themselves and create a more stable plant community. Annual meadows can be wonderfully bright and cheerful, although their glory lasts for only a few weeks. Not surprisingly, there are many gardeners who would like to re-create this colourful spectacle at home, but it is not the easiest wild flower community to keep going. For a garden 'cornfield' to be anything other than a nine-day wonder, you must be prepared for some hard work and good organization, making 'succession sowings' in the way that vegetable growers do (see page 85).

Cornfield wild flowers can also be sown with perennial wild flower mixes, providing a splash of colour in the first year before the perennial meadow gets into its stride. These annuals act as a 'nurse crop', offering temporary shelter for the slower-growing perennial seedlings. Temporary they may be, but their bold primary colours are undeniably striking.

Prairies

When the first European settlers arrived in North America the prairie swept on for thousands of miles, rolling lands of grass and wild flowers. Vast herds of buffalo grazed on the grasses, followed by the plains Indians who depended on their meat for food and their hides for clothing. The great plains have a harsh climate, cold in winter, hot in summer, with low rainfall and the ever-present danger of fire. Fire was the crucial factor that made the prairie a different kind of grassland to the meadows we have looked at so far. Fire stopped the growth of trees and scrub, making grasslands the 'natural' vegetation of the plains.

Today there is only about one per cent of the original tall-grass prairie left, as the great grasslands of the past have been planted with wheat and brought almost to the brink of extinction. But it is now the turn of the prairie to be expanded again, as a uniquely American experiment in landscaping has got under way. Since the 1930s botanists, landscapers and amateur gardeners have been re-creating prairies all over the mid-west, seeing in them an unrivalled form of low-maintenance planting, one that offers a constantly changing spectacle of wild

A recently established prairie planting is a sea of yellow coneflowers (Ratibida pinnata), *with michaelmas daisies* (Aster species) *and a few* Rudbeckia *species in the foreground. In years to come, the coneflowers will be largely replaced by a wider mixture of species.*

flowers and wildlife. Prairies and their wild flowers have also attracted interest from European garden designers and landscape architects, drawn by their practicality and the elegant majesty of prairie plants. The plant community native to prairies thrives in areas of low summer rainfall, and poor or difficult soils are no barrier to prairie success either.

Prairies through the seasons

The prairies are made up of a number of distinctive, and very attractive, species of grass, among which a wide variety of wild flowers flourish. To some extent the prairie has much in common with meadow habitats in other areas of North America, many of the plant species being the same. The unique quality of a prairie is that it is a naturally occurring meadow, which makes it a stable ecological system when established. The grasses and certain of the wild flowers, notably various members of the pea and daisy families (Leguminosae and Compositae), form a 'matrix', a thick tangle of roots and stems that makes it difficult for alien weeds to establish themselves, but at the same time provides ideal conditions for

LEFT *Mauve blazing star* (Liatris spicata) *and white rattlesnake-master* (Eryngium yuccifolium) *flower at mid-summer in this area of prairie. Rattlesnake-master also flourishes in coastal situations.*

FAR LEFT *Several species of michaelmas daisy* (Aster) *and goldenrod* (Solidago) *flower profusely in early autumn in prairie plantings. The yellow and purple make a dramatic colour combination. These late-flowering species can grow very tall, some to head height, and they spread vigorously, especially on fertile soils.*

other, less vigorous prairie wild flowers to grow.

In the spring the first flowers to show above the remnants of last year's dead herbage are small, less than 40cm (16in) high, and include shooting stars (*Dodecatheon meadia*), pasque flowers (*Pulsatilla patens*), violets (*Viola* species) and prairie smoke (*Geum triflorum*). As the season becomes warmer and the grasses get into their stride the next flowers are taller, up to 90cm (3ft), and include milkweeds (*Asclepias* species), columbines (*Aquilegia canadensis*), false indigos (*Baptisia* species), lupins (*Lupinus perennis*), coneflowers (*Echinacea* species) and coreopsis.

Towards the end of the summer the grasses and some of the wild flowers are taller than head height. It is the tall grasses and flowers of this season that make the prairie so distinctive, bringing together all those classic American wild flowers – the yellow daisies of sunflowers (*Helianthus* species), black-eyed susans (*Rudbeckia* species) and goldenrods (*Solidago* species), the great fuzzy pink heads of joe pye weed (*Eupatorium* species, including *E. fistulosum* and *E. purpureum*) and queen of the prairie (*Filipendula rubra*) and the vivid purples of ironweeds (*Vernonia* species) and blazing star (*Liatris* species). Magnificent plants in their own right are the tall-grass prairie grasses, which include big bluestem (*Andropogon gerardii*), indian grass (*Sorghastrum nutans*) and switch grass (*Panicum virgatum*). In the short-grass prairie, a plant community found further west, the dominant grasses are little bluestem (*Andropogon scoparius*) and side oats gramma (*Bouteloua curtipendula*).

With the arrival of autumn the grasses will turn red and copper and the flowers die away to leave their seedheads for the birds. Throughout the year a prairie is invaluable for wildlife, providing seeds for food in autumn and winter, nectar and breeding grounds for insects during spring and summer, and cover all year round.

Woodland shade

It could be said that woodland is the most natural vegetation there is. It covered most temperate areas of the globe until humans intervened. If a field, a garden or an area of waste ground were left, without being weeded or cut or grazed, it would eventually revert to woodland of some kind. Once trees are established, they are able to shade out other communities of plants, such as grasses and meadow flowers, and the only plants that can co-exist with them are those that can tolerate this shade. A brief comparison between wild flowers found in a meadow and those that are growing in a neighbouring wood, will reveal

by nature – indeed, their springtime glory is actually one of the survival strategies of shade-tolerant plants. They have adapted to start growing as early in the year as temperatures will allow, producing flowers and foliage before the trees overhead come into leaf. By the time the trees are in full leaf, most woodland wild flowers have completed the bulk of their year's work, which involves laying down food reserves and the process of reproduction.

Walking through different kinds of woodland soon reveals very different sorts of vegetation. Woods on fertile soils can have a dense, at times even

The wood anemones (Anemone nemorosa) on the left and the lesser celandines (Ranunculus ficaria) on the right are two of the earliest shade-loving wild flowers; they make a good juxtaposition to the foliage of the fern. Lesser celandine, in particular, spreads rapidly to colonize woodlands.

that they are different in many respects, woodlanders often having dark evergreen leaves, for instance. Shade plants cannot cope with the intense jostling for space that goes on in the sun, while sun-lovers in a wood grow weak and spindly, to be pushed aside by those better adapted for such conditions.

Many plants have adapted to woodland shade and have flourished to the extent that they provide some of our most beautiful floral sights. Springtime in a woodland in Europe means drifts of violets (*Viola* species), wood anemones (*Anemone nemorosa*), primroses (*Primula vulgaris*) and, most spectacular of all, bluebells (*Hyacinthoides non-scripta*). The traditional harbingers of spring are nearly all woodland plants

impenetrable, quite tall ground cover of brambles, ferns and larger woody shrubs such as hazel (*Corylus avellana*). The richer and more moist the soil, the better most plants will generally grow, so that the soil's condition, to some extent, offsets the effects of shade. Plants that require light grow more strongly, even in deep shade, on a fertile soil or a moist site than in conditions of dry shade on a poor soil. There are many lovely plants that will flourish in moist shade, but few that relish or even tolerate dry shade (see page 57). Woods on poorer, and acid, soils will be easier to walk through. There is less vegetation altogether, more moss, and a lighter cover of dwarf shrubs, small ferns and light grasses.

RIGHT *Woodlands provide some of our most spectacular wild flower sights. Foxgloves* (Digitalis purpurea) *in a variety of colours have self-sown in this area of light shade on acid soil. Although individual plants usually die after flowering, biennial foxgloves generally grow and spread vigorously, becoming a permanent presence because of the large quantity of seed they produce to start off the next generation. Here they are seen against the large rounded, glossy leaves of a bergenia.*

LEFT *Clump-forming primroses* (Primula vulgaris) *are a familiar feature in many woodlands from late winter to late spring. Once planted they will slowly spread by seeding.*

Types of woodland

The kind of wild flower community to be found in forests and woodlands is determined by the predominant trees, the soil's level of acidity or alkalinity and, above all, by its moisture level.

The trees Some trees are not only extremely well adapted to catching most of the sun's light as it comes to earth, but also at extracting moisture and nutrients from the ground. Many conifers, beeches (*Fagus* species) and maples such as European sycamore (*Acer pseudoplatanus*) come into this category, and there is very little that can be persuaded to grow directly underneath them. But as long as natural conifer forests are fairly open, they can support some wild flowers, such as cowberry (*Vaccinium vitis-idaea*), wood rushes (*Luzula* species) and cow-wheat (*Melampyrum sylvaticum*). Closely spaced trees mean a dark woodland floor where little beyond mosses and specialized wild flowers like wintergreen (*Pyrola* species) will thrive. On the other hand, certain trees, for example birches (*Betula* species), cast such a light shade that many sun-lovers will grow beneath them,

Dog's tooth violet or trout lily (Erythronium dens-canis) and wild daffodil (Narcissus pseudonarcissus) flower beneath an oak tree. Lesser celandine (Ranunculus ficaria) flowers in front. The colours of shade-tolerant flowers can be as spectacular as those of sun-loving species.

Early in spring wood anemones (Anemone nemorosa), left, and Cyclamen repandum, right, flower together in light shade beneath the trees. Both will spread, slowly but surely, over the years. The leaf litter provides an effective mulch, conserving moisture in the soil.

such as bilberry (*Vaccinium myrtillus*) and heather (*Calluna vulgaris*). As a general rule, the deeper the shade, the more restricted plant growth will be.

Soil acidity or alkalinity Many natural woodlands have a slightly acid soil, and some of the most delightful wild flowers need acid conditions to thrive. In a woodland with acid soil conditions you will find the larger shrubby dogwoods (*Cornus* species), wild rhododendrons and azaleas, with possibly a forest-floor planting of trilliums, shortias and creeping phlox. Woodlands on a limy (alkaline) soil tend to have more lush vegetation on the ground. Woodruff (*Galium odoratum*), wood spurge (*Euphorbia amygdaloides*) bellflowers (*Campanula* species) and hellebores all enjoy an alkaline shady site.

Degree of moisture The limited selection of plants that can cope with dry shade conditions include the male fern (*Dryopteris filix-mas*) and the evergreen christmas fern (*Polystichium acrostichoides*), as well as

the alum roots (*Heuchera* species) and the related *Tellima grandiflora*, a group of plants with attractive rosettes of evergreen leaves and white or green flowers. Periwinkles (*Vinca minor* and *V. major*), evergreen trailers with blue flowers, will also grow in dry shade, as will the redoutable *Euphorbia robbiae*, a strongly spreading evergreen plant with attractive pale green flowers in early spring. The ultimate survivor for dry shady places is ivy (*Hedera helix*).

In damp woodlands many ferns grow luxuriantly, creating a cool, soothing atmosphere, including the ostrich fern (*Matteucia struthiopteris*), with light green arching fronds and the lower-growing sensitive fern (*Onoclea sensibilis*). If the shade is not too dense you will find flowering plants such as meadowsweet (*Filipendula ulmaria*) and goat's beard (*Aruncus dioicus*), a magnificent plant with distinctive ribbed leaves that can grow to 2m (6½ft); both have soft, creamy flowerheads in summer that consort well with delicate fern foliage. Bugle (*Ajuga reptans*) makes an excellent ground cover for damp shade.

The intensity of bluebells (Hyacinthoides non-scripta) in flower is a magnificent sight. This most spectacular of wild flowers covers the ground in many a northern European woodland with a carpet of shimmering blue in late spring. Luckily for the gardener they are easy to establish in part-shade, especially on lighter soils.

Half-shade

In areas of partial shade, where there is more light all year round, a wider variety of wild flowers and grasses, as well as shrubs, can be found, including more summer-flowering species. Most of the true woodlanders cannot grow here because the taller and more vigorous plants that do well under light shade crowd them out, although hedges and small areas of tree cover vary so much in density that there are sure to be dark places where real shade-lovers will still thrive. Woodland borders and forest clearings are important places for wildlife as well as wild flowers, offering a half-way house between open fields and woodland, with the density of shrubs and climbers providing safe places to roost and breed.

Hedgerows

The secret of the hedge environment is that it can offer a rich variety of micro-habitats in a very small space, both horizontally and vertically. The year may start with snowdrops and primroses in the shadiest

RIGHT *Spring-flowering species in light shade can be very colourful; yellow archangel (Lamiastrum galeobdolon), bugle (Ajuga reptans) and red campion (Silene dioica) all thrive in slightly moist sites. The thistle would need to be removed to prevent competition.*

ABOVE Geranium *'Johnson's Blue' is a hardy geranium cultivar that looks appropriate alongside wild flowers. Here it grows next to a snowy woodrush (Luzula nivea), flowering in mid-summer, in an area of part-shade.*

RIGHT *The best time of year for hedgerow wild flowers is late spring. Here red campion, buttercups (Ranunculus arvensis) and wild garlic (Allium ursinum) grow in the shade at the base of a hedge. Wild garlic grows and flowers rapidly in spring, dying back to bulbs by mid-summer.*

areas at the foot of the hedge. In late spring, many hedges are a mass of pink, white and blue. The ubiquitous red campion (*Silene dioica*) contributes the pink, bluebells the blue and the white is provided by greater stitchwort (*Stellaria holostea*) and cow parsley (*Anthriscus sylvestris*) and its relatives. Flowering shrubs such as hawthorn (*Crataegus monogyna*) and viburnums may form part of the hedge itself. The arrival of summer will see taller wild flowers such as the butter-yellow st john's wort (*Hypericum perforatum*) and wild roses. Other colourful wild flowers that will keep a hedge bright for months to come include the pink herb-robert (*Geranium robertianum*) and the more showy wood cranesbill (*G. sylvaticum*), and several dead-nettles: yellow archangel (*Lamium galeobdolon*), white dead-nettle (*L. album*) and spotted dead-nettle (*L. maculatum*). Late summer in a country hedge can be a rather flowerless time, although the devil's bit scabious (*Succisa pratensis*) will be in flower and much appreciated by butterflies. The later months can be colourful with berries and the rich tints of autumn foliage.

Woodland glades

Open areas in woodland, forest glades and the borders of woods and forest, although less diverse ecologically, still have much to offer. This is the habitat favoured by one of the most spectacular of all springtime wild flowers, the bluebell. And when spring turns imperceptibly into summer, you may see several other woodland glade species, with flowers on tall stems held clear above the foliage. The biennial foxglove is one of the best known, and another is the monkshood, the most familiar species being *Aconitum napellus*, a dark, glossy purple; there are also others, *Aconitum vulparia* with pale yellow flowers or the climbing *Aconitum volubile*, with paler mauve flowers. Campanulas are an attractive group of tall, shade-tolerant wild flowers: nettle-leaved bellflower (*Campanula trachelium*), a pretty shade of pale grey-blue, and the much darker giant bellflower (*C. latifolia*) both self-seed easily. The tallest flower spikes are those of the cimicifugas: *Cimicifuga racemosa* and *C. cordifolia* send their slender spikes of white flowers up to a metre high, while the autumn-flowering *C. simplex* grows taller still.

Wetlands

Of all habitats, wetlands are some of the best endowed. The ecology of a wetland is richer than a comparable area of dry land, since besides the large number of plants and animals that it can support within its boundaries, a wetland benefits a wider area by attracting birds and insects that come there to feed and drink. Take a walk down to an unspoilt riverside, reed bed or pond on a hot day, and simply listen to the constant background buzz of insects.

Marshes and ponds

Within two or three years a new area of damp meadow will look as though it has always been there, since plant life as well as animal life establishes quickly in a wetland, the constant supply of moisture ensuring that growth never ceases through the spring and summer. The year may start off with the bright yellow of kingcups, and the white and yellow

The yellow kingcups (Caltha palustris) and the long-stalked panicles of the umbrella plant (Darmera peltata) are two of the earliest waterside plants to flower. Later in spring the large leaves of the umbrella plant will unfold.

spathes of the bog arums or skunk cabbage (*Lysichiton* species), but it is in the summer that most moisture-lovers really get into their stride. Colours are often vibrant, with the dark magenta of purple loosestrifes (*Lythrum salicaria*) and a lot of strong yellows, such as yellow flag irises (*Iris pseudacorus*), and yellow loosestrifes (*Lysimachia* species). North American wetlands can be even more colourful, with rich purple water

irises (*I. versicolor* and *I. virginica*) and brilliant scarlet cardinal flowers (*Lobelia cardinalis*). But there are many subtle moisture-loving flowers as well, including meadowsweets with their enchanting scent, soft pink hemp agrimony and joe pye weeds as well as the innumerable grass-like plants that do well by water, such as common reeds (*Phragmites australis*), reedmace (*Typha latifolia*) and soft rush (*Juncus effusus*). The grasses and sedges may be subtle in colouring, but their strength is in their form, especially that of their seedheads which will often last throughout the winter season.

There are degrees in any habitat, degrees of shade and of fertility, but it is the degree of moisture that gives the greatest variation in plant life. A graduation from dry land to water is usual in the wild and this provides a number of different habitats for a broad spectrum of wild flowers.

A merely damp meadow area is usually lush with some wild flowers that you tend not to find in drier places, such as globeflowers (*Trollius* species), ladies' smocks (*Cardamine pratensis*) and ragged robins (*Lychnis flos-cuculi*). Where the ground becomes really soggy, the flora changes again, with kingcups, pale yellow water avens (*Geum rivale*) and fluffy pink water mint (*Mentha aquatica*). At the water's edge you find a distinctive flora, the so-called 'marginal' or 'emergent' plants that are happy to root under water, including water irises, reedmace (*Typha latifolia*) and the pink-flowering rush (*Butomus umbellatus*). Kingcups and loosestrifes will flourish with their feet in water too.

In the water itself there are truly aquatic plants like water-lilies and the various hidden underwater plants that play such a vital role in oxygenating the water of a pond. Water-lilies are essential in water, not only aesthetically but also because their leaves provide shade for pond life and play an important part in pond ecology. But their beauty should not blind us to the other, smaller wild flowers which may be found in a small pond, such as the bogbean (*Menyanthes trifoliata*), with its highly distinctive pink-fringed petals, or the water violet.

A pond with a variety of waterside plants growing beside it. Water-lilies (Nymphaea) *dominate the water itself, while the quietly spectacular flowering rush (Butomus umbellatus), with pink flowers on tall stems, grows out of the water where it is shallower. Yellow loosestrife (Lysimachia punctata) forms a bold clump in front of the flowering rush, in the wet soil at the edge of the pond.*

The water violet (Hottonia palustris) *has underwater leaves but flowers above water in summer with its pretty pale mauve or whitish flowers. It prefers cool, clear water, running or still.*

Streams, riversides, bogs

The banks of streams and rivers are potentially some of the loveliest places to find wild flowers growing. The sight and sound of running water make a background that is at once lively and restful. Plants with big, dramatic foliage like the various butterburs (*Petasites* species) with large, rounded leaves or those with stems or leaves that arch out over the water such as the weeping sedge (*Carex pendula*) often clothe river banks to great effect.

The sides of streams are frequently shaded by overhanging trees, in which case you will find shade-tolerant plants such as ferns. If the site is open and sunny, any of the wetland wild flowers will thrive (see page 60). Marginal plants such as yellow flags (*Iris pseudacorus*) are usually found lower down, where there is a danger of at least seasonal flooding, with

marshland species like meadowsweet (*Filipendula ulmaria*) or hemp agrimony (*Eupatorium cannabinum*) further up. Other attractive and quick to establish streamside plants include blue forget-me-nots (*Myosotis laxa* and *M. scorpioides*) and monkey flowers (*Mimulus* species), which have yellow or red flowers. It has to be said, though, that these two, along with several other waterside plants, such as the notorious lizard tails (*Saururus cernuus*), can spread very fast; this may be fine in the larger garden but potentially overwhelming in a small plot.

A bank is often unstable so strong-growing plants with hefty root systems can play a vital role in holding it all together. A first-rate bank protector is *Peltiphyllum peltatum*, whose extraordinary pink flowers appear in the year before the leaves, which are large and dramatic. Another vigorously rooting plant found on the higher reaches of a river bank is

the bistort (*Polygonum bistorta*), which has attractive pale pink flower spikes in early summer.

Bogs

Water levels are the main variable of wetland habitats, as we have seen. Another important one is the acidity or alkalinity of the soil and water, which has a dramatic effect on the flora of a wetland area. Wetlands in alkaline – that is, lime-rich – regions look lush, burgeoning with fertility, full of tall, waving reeds and vigorous, colourful wild flowers like the irises and loosestrifes mentioned above. At first glance acid wetlands, properly called bogs, are distinctly poorer than those in alkaline soils; they are less brightly coloured and have a less richly developed fauna. But on closer examination their distinct wild flower flora contains some extraordinary plants and a bog garden can be surprisingly colourful.

Two particularly bold plants are the spring-flowering swamp pinks (*Helonias bullata*) and the bright pink meadow beauties (*Rhexia virginica*) which flowers in late summer. Bog plants are almost all lime-haters so a bog garden is only feasible where there is no danger of lime getting into the water. The fertility of a bog needs to be kept low so that weedier grasses and sedges do not flourish. Since bog plants have adapted to live in what is quite a hostile environment for most plants, they cannot compete with strong growers on a richer soil. Bogs are so poor in nitrogen that some plants have adapted to eating insects to get this mineral; cool-climate bogs will support several species of sundew (*Drosera* species) which capture insects on specially adapted sticky leaves, whereas the bog in a warmer climate can have a wider variety of carnivorous plants such as the pitcher plants (*Sarracenia* species).

Next to the waterside, two iris species enjoy the constant moisture. Yellow flag iris (Iris pseudacorus) *is a robust and adaptable species, native to Europe, which has naturalized in North America. Next to it is the purple-flowered* Iris ensata *from Japan, a fine species, but one that needs lime-free soil and water.*

Heathlands

Heaths and moors are all too often thought of as barren wastes, blasted by wind and driving rain. These acid, infertile soils support few plants other than rhododendrons, azaleas and heathers. But when the heather is in full bloom, heaths can be one of the most colourful of all habitats. Rooting around in the heather can reveal a wealth of other plants too, many of them closely related to heather – wiry little shrubs like bilberry (*Vaccinium myrtillus*) and bog rosemary (*Andromeda polifolia*). These dwarf shrubs are nearly always tangled up with each other, their stems so intertwined that it is impossible to see where one plant begins and another ends.

If you have a site with this somewhat inhospitable soil, a heath garden may be the most successful kind of planting. It will have the advantage of being undemanding in its maintenance requirements, since its low-growing, tightly knit habit means that it will need little cutting or weeding. What you can grow in a heath garden is largely determined by the local climate. If it is really cold and desolate in winter, then only the hardiest plants will survive. Fortunately, there is a huge number of cultivars of the hardiest lings and heathers (*Calluna vulgaris, Erica carnea* and *E. cinerea*) to choose from; unlike most plant cultivars, many of these are simply selections found in the wild. *Calluna vulgaris* turns many heathlands a deep purple in the later summer months, and makes what many regard as the finest honey. *Erica carnea* is usefully late-winter flowering and, for a heather, it is surprisingly lime-tolerant. Tough little shrubs like the cowberry (*Vaccinium vitis-idaea*), with its bright red berries, and the bearberry (*Arctostaphylos uva-ursi*), a glossy-leaved trailer, will grow in and out of the heather, contrasting in leaf form.

Some other low-growing shrubs that belong to the heather/rhododendron family, such as *Gaultheria*, are able to cope with high winds and thin soils. These are relatives of the bilberries and blueberries, wiry shrubs with attractive foliage and berries. The well-known bilberry (*Vaccinium myrtillus*) may not be the most exciting member of this group, but it will grow in the most exposed and wind-blasted of places, and its fruit are deliciously edible. The juniper (*Juniperus communis*) and the common broom (*Cytisus scoparius*), a shrub with bright yellow pea flowers, are two of the toughest taller plants for cold places. Another versatile shrub is the pepper bush (*Clethra alnifolia*), with sweetly scented white flowers. There are also some attractive grasses tolerant of these conditions, such as the purple moor grass (*Molinia caerulea*).

Some areas of heathland have a blustery but quite mild climate. They offer growing conditions suitable for a much wider range of plants, again many of them members of the heather family (Ericaceae). Some heathers from the Mediterranean area are quite spectacular, such as st daboec's heath (*Daboecia cantabrica*) with its plump mauve bells, the cornish heath (*Erica vagans*) which grows up to a metre and the white-flowered tree heather (*Erica arborea*), which grows up to three times as high. A few other heathland shrubs grow taller in areas of mild climate; these include various brooms and the strawberry tree (*Arbutus unedo*), named for its red fruit, which will grow to tree size in a sheltered location.

Hardy heathers (including Erica erigena) flower in the acid soil of a heathland garden, interspersed by the taller Juniperus species and, behind, the yellow-flowering broom (Cytisus scoparius).

Dry areas

Spring brings colour to many dry regions, as plants flower before the heat of the summer. Here a broom (Cytisus species) flowers among French lavender (Lavandula stoechas). In areas like this, with a Mediterranean climate, many wild flowers make the most of their growth in the period from autumn to spring.

Contrary to popular opinion, dry-zone plants are not just austere greys and browns, but are able to give us some of the most spectacular floral displays on earth. The native flora of Australia is one of the world's richest and most beautiful, for example. The glorious banksias, melaleucas, grevilleas and other wild flowers of the bush are becoming increasingly popular garden plants outside Australia.

Dry climates vary considerably of course and so do the plants that grow in them. But certain characteristics recur frequently among the plants, be it in the Australian outback, the French maquis or the Californian chaparral; plants with small, grey drought-resistant leaves, often hairy or waxy and containing aromatic oils, tough, wiry little shrubs, and trees with flaky, fireproof bark. Several of the shrubby Mediterranean plants that have been in cultivation for centuries are of this type: lavender, myrtle, sage and cistus. Drier still are semi-desert areas where plants have water-storing succulent foliage or underground tubers, and a population of dramatically bright annuals that carpet the land with colour after the rains. Selecting the best plants for garden use is the pioneering task of the dry-zone wild flower gardener.

Dry-climate habitats tend to be composed of fewer trees and herbaceous plants and more shrubs, bulbs and annuals. The most characteristic trees of dry regions are pines, olive trees (*Olea europaea*) and species of *Arbutus*. Many dry regions have a rich bulb flora which takes advantage of the cool, moist conditions of winter to grow and to flower, retreating underground before the summer's heat. Wild tulip species, including *Tulipa sylvestris*, display a huge variety of colours and shapes. The wild anemones, such as *Anemone pavonina*, from the Mediterranean region are another boldly coloured group of plants with underground storage organs. Shrubs and what herbaceous plants there are may well flower in the cool season too, leaving annuals as the chief source of summer colour. The annual flora of dry regions is often very rich, but lies hidden as scattered seeds for much of the time. In south-western parts of North America, species such as desert sand verbena (*Abronia villosa*), desert marigold (*Baileya multiradiata*) and californian bluebells (*Phacelia campanularia*) are very colourful after the rains.

Coastal areas

Living by the sea is an attractive prospect in many ways but while we can shelter indoors when the winter storms pound the coast, or the sun blazes down for days on end, plants have to cope with whatever the elements bring them. Coastal sites have a lot to contend with: hot sun, accompanied by desiccating winds in summer, followed by winter gales, in which the salt-laden wind can do much damage to soft plant tissue. Seaside soils are usually infertile, either very dry or waterlogged, and sometimes both in quick succession. These conditions are some of the most trying to garden in but, fortunately for the gardener, there is a wide range of attractive seashore wild flowers that have adapted themselves to these harsh conditions.

There are two main coastal habitats: the shore itself, where the wind and salt-spray impose great limitations on what will grow, and the often erratically drained sandy soils further inland where there is more shelter. Plants that live on the front line with the sea often have thick, waxy leaves that protect them from desiccation and salt. Some well-adapted plants that would cope with a rock garden or small border by the seaside are thrift, sea campion and the oyster plant (*Mertensia maritima*), whose leaves are covered in a beautiful glaucous bloom and which has pure blue forget-me-not flowers in spring. Somewhat larger plants include the sea holly, sea lavenders (*Limonium* species), with sprays of pink flowers, and sea pea (*Lathyrus japonicus*), a pink relative of the

LEFT *The steely blue of sea holly* (Eryngium maritimum) *echoes the blue of the sea in the background. This unusual and beautiful wild flower, with its bluish leaves and spiky, thistle-like flowers, is one of a select few that can flourish in shifting sands, a hostile environment for most plants.*

sweet pea. Few shrubs thrive by the sea, but some of the best flowering shrubs that do are the burnet rose (*Rosa pimpinellifolia*), tamarisk (*Tamarix* species) and the spectacular pink tree mallow (*Lavatera arborea*).

Drifting sand is one of the problems the seaside gardener may have to face. Fortunately there are some tough grasses that will bind the sand together and even grow back up through a considerable depth of sand if they get buried. The European marram grass (*Ammophila arenaria*) is one of the best for holding unstable sand dunes together, but it is not in the top league for its ornamental qualities. North Americans have two native species that are good-looking too: sea oats (*Uniola paniculata*) and beach panic grass (*Panicum amarum*). Grasses look especially good by the sea, their vertical lines offering a contrast to the overwhelming sense of the horizontal that one feels in maritime landscapes.

Further away from the coast itself, among the dunes, there is a variety of wild flowers that does well. The mallow family (Malvaceae) includes several big, lusty growers with large pink flowers that thrive where drainage is poor: marsh mallow (*Althaea officinalis*), seashore mallow (*Kosteletskya virginica*) and some species of hibiscus. There are various daisy relatives that grow well, such as fleabane (*Pulicaria dysentrica*) and blanket flower (*Gaillardia pulchella*). The tall, vigorous-growing evening primroses (*Oenothera* species) thrive in sand too, presenting a cheerful sight among the dunes.

Despite the wind and salt spray, the coast can be a colourful wild flower habitat. Growing on the cliffs here are thrift (Armeria maritima), *forming dense cushions covered in papery, soft pink flower clusters, sea campion* (Silene maritima), *a strong spreader with white flowers, and* Carpobrotus deliciosus, *a South African species with pink flowers.*

ESTABLISHING WILD FLOWER HABITATS

Creating a wild flower habitat is both a joy and a challenge and can entail a radically different approach to garden making. Wild flower gardens or areas involve as much time and effort as do other kinds of garden, and will require care while the plants are establishing, but once mature they need little long-term maintenance. They cannot be made simply by sowing a packet of seed and hoping for the best; the establishment of a stable plant community may take several years, although there will be plenty to look at and enjoy in the meantime.

Mauve corncockles (Agrostemma githago) *and poppies* (Papaver rhoeas) *border a path of mown grass, with a lush display of flowers. They are both annuals, which means they will need re-seeding every spring to look as good as this every year. Among them however is a little yellow* Thermopsis *which, being perennial, will return every year.*

Preparing the site

The most important task in creating wild flower habitats in a garden is that of weed control. There are many plants, undesirable in the garden, which are so strong-growing or which reproduce so rapidly, that they will make it difficult to grow the wild flowers we want if they are not eradicated. Among them are several kinds of grass that tend to suffocate anything else growing around them; one of these is agricultural rye grass (*Lolium perenne* cultivars), often included in garden lawn mixtures. Other familiar ones are docks (*Rumex* species), stinging nettle (*Urtica dioica*) and fat-hen (*Chenopodium album*). The ability of these tough 'weed' species to lurk in the ground, as seed or pieces of buried root, is quite amazing. Ensuring a clean, weed-free start to your wild flower garden is a task that can never be hurried and it requires great patience. It is time-consuming enough weeding a conventional flower border or a line of cabbages, but weeding a meadow is a thousand times worse – believe me, I have done it!

If the area you will be planting has been well cultivated previously, there should not be too much of a weed problem. The soil surface need only be turned over and prepared for planting or seed sowing (see pages 76–83). Areas of lawn that are being converted to wild flower meadow need to be treated with some caution, however, as they might contain a lot of rye grass. The lawn grass can be stripped off with a spade and taken away for composting. The site can then be left bare for a few weeks to see if any of the grass regenerates from deep runners; if it does, the site needs to be dug over to remove grass roots.

Areas that are covered in weeds or other unwanted vegetation obviously have to be completely cleared. But there is something of a dilemma with areas of semi-natural vegetation that you want to 'improve' or enrich with more wild flowers. For instance, you may have a rather neglected field that, in your mind's eye, would make a lovely wild flower meadow. Do you clear patches and sow seed of the wild flowers you want, or do you start again from scratch? It is a common problem because often we wish to plant wild flowers in areas that are semi-natural to start

with. Many areas of rough ground have a mixture of desirable grasses and wild flowers as well as undesirable weed species (see page 72). There may be patches of turf containing some of the wild flowers you want to establish, but then there may be patches of thistles or nettles or swathes of what appear to be nothing but tough pasture grasses.

There are two quite different approaches when you are faced with such a site. One is the drastic approach, of obliterating everything and starting again from scratch, and the other is to try and improve what is there. Both have their potential dangers. You will have to decide first which are the 'weeds' and assess how widespread they are; which wild flowers are already there, how many species, and are there any which are uncommon in your area? One of the joys, and sometimes one of the challenges, of wild flower gardening is that it is an experimental science, with too many variables or unknowns to make hard and fast judgements on courses of action. But having assessed the situation, you may prefer not to commit yourself and to treat several plots in different ways.

Improving what exists

If there is a good selection of wild flowers on your site, this probably indicates that there is not a great weed problem and it would be absurd to clear the ground and start from scratch. However, if the weeds *are* widespread, and you still decide to improve the site, rather than start again, for whatever reason, then you may have to spend time on selective weed control (see pages 72–3).

Improving the site can be tackled in several ways. First it will be necessary to deal with the perennial weeds by hand digging or spot spraying (see page 73). Most weeds, in my experience, make it easier for you by growing in patches rather than distributing themselves evenly. You may then clear small areas for sowing or planting and eventually the wild flowers will spread out from these initial plantings. A more drastic alternative is to cut the existing vegetation down low and rotovate it (see page 72), but this would be unsatisfactory in areas with a perennial-weed problem or which are covered in rye grass. Wild flowers may then be sown and will blend in with the existing vegetation as it regenerates. This approach carries the risk of damaging the existing flora, however, as the most vigorous existing species will be the main beneficiaries.

Starting from scratch

If your site is bereft of wild flowers and certainly if there are many perennial weeds, including rye grass, then you will probably have to adopt the drastic approach. The advantage of this is that you will be able to start with a clean slate. A possible disadvantage manifests itself if you meet obstacles halfway through; then, with the local balance of nature disturbed, new problems may arise, and you will wish you had never started clearing the site in the first place. I am thinking in particular of two problems here. One is the mass germination of dormant weed seed that has hitherto been safely buried and out of harm's way. The other problem can be that the very toughest weeds may survive any treatment you adopt and, with the competition dead or cleared away, will take complete control.

The germination of dormant weed seed can be dealt with by leaving the land fallow after turning it over and killing what comes up. Indeed, if you are going to sow rather than plant, and especially if there is a large area to be sown, scattered with only annual weeds, then it is often possible to get away with one shallow cultivation. Perennial weeds can be sprayed with a glyphosate-based weedkiller, then removed by slicing through them horizontally with a spade just below soil level (done with surprising ease after glyphosate treatment), and the soil surface rotovated or dug to a depth of a few centimetres only. The weed seed present in the top layer of soil will germinate, but the rest will stay safely buried. Once you have sprayed or hoed these weed seedlings, you will be ready to sow. An alternative is to use black plastic (see page 72) over one growing season and to cultivate and sow the following year.

The second problem, that of highly resistant weeds, notably horsetail (*Equisetum arvense*), is best approached realistically. You will have to accept that you are always going to have some horsetail and put up with it, because if you try to get rid of it by digging and forking, this will break up the extensive root system and stimulate the development of many more of the weeds. In the end, you may have nothing but horsetail. Having tried to get rid of it, I write these words from bitter experience.

A neglected garden like this will probably contain a mixture of overgrown garden plants, as well as weeds and some desirable wild flowers. Deciding what to clear and what to keep is one of the first major decisions the gardener has to take.

Clearing weedy ground

There is a variety of techniques that can be used to clear ground infested with weeds and unwanted vegetation. The conventional way is to use weed-killers, which are generally efficient, although they do not deal with buried weed seed. Organic gardeners use a number of other techniques (see below), which can be just as effective over a longer time scale and should be considered. The kind of weeds that you have – annual weeds or shallow- or deep-rooted perennials – will to some extent determine the best method to use. Perennial weeds have deep roots or branched, horizontal rooting systems that are difficult to remove. Annual weeds – plants like fat-hen (*Chenopodium*), chickweed (*Stellaria*) and petty spurge (*Euphorbia peplus*) – often look worse than they are. They grow rapidly on bare soil but, being shallow-rooted, can easily be hoed off, which should be done as soon as you see them, so that they cannot seed and start off another generation.

Hand digging The traditional and somewhat pains-taking method is simply to dig over the land, removing weed plants and roots. Digging to the depth of a spit (the depth of the spade blade) is adequate to get out most weeds; deeper-rooted specimens will need following down to remove the entire root. This can take ages, and its effectiveness can be limited as it is impossible to spot every little piece of root, especially of couch grass (*Agropyron repens*) and some deep-rooted weeds such as bindweed (*Convolvulus* species).

Digging can be done repeatedly, the site being left alone for some time in between so that any remaining roots can resprout and be dug out, and any germinating seedlings hoed off. This takes time, but there is no doubt about its environmental safety. But for areas too large to hand dig, or for those who want quicker results, the following methods are a more realistic proposition.

Rotovating Land can be rotovated in a process that chops up weeds, but it leaves pieces of root in the soil which can re-sprout. The process needs to be carried out several times over the course of one growing season to be effective against such persistent perennials as couch grass and dock. Rotovators can easily be hired, but in my opinion they are heavy and difficult to handle, and while useful for turning over light weeds and weed-free land prior to sowing, they are not the best tool for the control of problem weeds. They can also damage the soil structure, especially that of heavier soils.

Hoeing This is a useful technique to clear the ground of annual weeds or seedlings. However, if the soil has much weed seed in it, the hoeing, like rotovating, needs to be done several times over a season, each time the latest crop of seedlings is a few centimetres high. This will eventually exhaust the supply of seed in the top layer of soil. Be careful to cultivate only the top few centimetres in preparing a seedbed or ground for planting (see page 76).

Black plastic Here is a method that works wonders with perennial weeds. Heavy-duty black plastic is rolled out over the soil in early spring, before growth has seriously started, and is weighted down round the edges. Weeds will start to grow underneath but will die from lack of light and by the autumn the land will usually be clear. You will have to check that the plastic stays in place, especially during any windy spells. The only weed that survives this treatment is horsetail, which will need two seasons under the plastic. Weed seeds will also remain alive under the plastic, but since these will mostly be shallow-rooted annuals they are less of a problem. Black plastic is relatively cheap, but it is not always possible to re-use it if it has too many holes or tears, which means that it has to be disposed of, preferably by burning, so that it does not end up on a landfill site. It burns surprisingly cleanly.

Solarizing This is a variant of the black plastic technique, best suited to warm climates. Black plastic is spread out and the edges buried so that a seal is formed. The heat of the sun is trapped underneath and the top layer of soil is effectively sterilized. The process is fast, taking only six weeks in the height of the summer. Deep tap-rooted weeds might still survive, however.

PERENNIAL WEEDS

Cirsium species (thistles) Digging is only partly effective; black plastic works well.

Equisetum (horsetail) Consider living with it! Or it takes two years of black plastic or sodium chlorate weedkiller.

Rumex (dock) Docks are susceptible to glyphosate weedkillers or can be dug up. Each plant has one taproot.

Urtica dioica (nettles) Nettles can be totally eradicated by careful digging or the black plastic method. But a small patch will benefit local butterflies.

Using weedkillers This is far and away the easiest method, although not acceptable to all gardeners. Advice on appropriate and safe weedkillers should always be sought from an agricultural advisory service or specialist garden sundries outlet. Many weedkillers leave harmful residues or will poison micro-organisms and invertebrates, but those based on glyphosate are relatively safe, as the chemical is rapidly bio-degraded in soil (but not in water, so great care must be exercised in using it near open water). Glyphosate is carried through the root system of a plant and is highly effective on grasses with runners, such as couch (*Agropyron repens*), docks and many perennial weeds; nettles (*Urtica dioica*) and some thistles (*Cirsium* species) will survive its use, however. The level of earthworm activity I have noticed under glyphosate-sprayed weeds is probably a good measure of its relative safety. Since glyphosate-resistant weeds will most often be found in localized patches, they can be dealt with by physical means, repeated digging or black plastic, albeit over a longer time scale.

The traditional ground-clearing weedkiller is sodium chlorate, which leaves the soil effectively poisoned for at least six months afterwards. I would recommend it only for controlling serious infestations of horsetail, which is resistant to anything else that the agrochemical industry produces; even then it takes two years of treatment to kill horsetail.

When using any weedkillers, wear protective clothing such as rubber gloves and boots, and wash them down afterwards. Ensure that no spray drifts on to other areas of your garden or on to neighbouring properties or open water. Common sense dictates that spraying is carried out in wind-free conditions as far as possible. Always read the manufacturer's instructions carefully and follow them precisely, with regard to rates of application and when to apply the weedkiller in question.

Even to the wild flower gardener, some species are still regarded as 'weeds'. Docks (Rumex species), here run to seed, thistles (Cirsium species) and ragwort (Senecio jacobaea) are vigorous, making it hard to establish more attractive wild flowers.

Spot-spraying

Regenerating perennial weeds or small patches of annual weeds can be spot-sprayed with a glyphosate-based weedkiller and left, to avoid disturbing the soil. The surrounding grass and wild flower seedlings will very soon grow over the dead vegetation. Where the weeds are growing among established plants or transplants, you must be particularly careful to spray only in wind-free conditions; keep the spray head as close to the target as possible and watch out for stray drips when you are moving around.

One refinement is to spray down through an empty plastic bottle from which the bottom has been cut off.

You can apply a mixture of weedkiller and wallpaper paste with a brush to ensure that the herbicide stays where it is put.

Soil fertility

Conventional gardening can involve spending considerable time and money on trying to change soils, with the addition of composts, soil conditioners and fertilizers. Wild flower gardening, on the other hand, should mean that the gardener works with nature, finding the right plants for the soil and site, rather than the other way round.

The paradox of wild flower gardening is that it is often better to have a rather infertile soil. Fertile soils, rather than encouraging all species to grow better, work to the advantage of those plants that can utilize the extra nutrients most effectively. This means that quick-growing grasses like cocksfoot (*Dactylis glomerata*) and vigorous wild flowers such as yarrow (*Achillea millefolium*) and ox-eye daisies (*Leucanthemum vulgare*) thrive, while the more delicate plants simply get swamped. This is why the richest or most interesting wild flower communities are often found on the poorest soils, such as the thin soils that are most commonly found over limestone or chalk downland (see page 49).

While it is still best to avoid vigorous grasses in poor soils, stronger-growing wild flowers, such as ox-eye daisy, are usually controllable in soils with low nutrient levels and will co-exist happily with fragile species like the harebell (*Campanula rotundiflora*). And if you want a good mix of wild flowers,

especially in a highly competitive environment like a meadow, then low fertility is a positive advantage. The need to keep fertility down is the reason that clippings should be removed when meadows and wild flower lawns are mown. You should not add any fertilizer or compost in any form either, unless perhaps you know the soil to be virtually pure sand!

Reducing soil fertility

If you suspect that weeds may be a problem or that the soil is naturally very fertile, it may even be worth considering reducing the fertility of your soil – the exact opposite of what gardeners are used to doing. There are several ways in which this can be done, besides simply removing the fertile layer, or the topsoil, as shown below.

Growing manure crops This involves adapting a technique used by organic growers who are trying to build up their soil fertility. Rapid-growing, leafy, nitrogen-greedy crops are planted in spring and then removed at maturity – that is, just before they seed. The conventional gardener would plough them in to rot down as compost, but the wild flower gardener needs to remove them from the site, together with the nutrients they have taken up. They can be composted to use on the rest of the garden or donated to other gardeners. The best crop to use in cooler climates is agricultural beet.

Topsoil stripping

If you have the equipment or the muscle power, this method of reducing soil fertility is a viable option. You can either remove the topsoil entirely, by taking off the darker, more friable layer, distinguishable in colour and texture from the subsoil beneath. Or you can simply strip off the top 10–20cm (4–8in), which will remove the main reservoir of nutrients, as well as weed seeds. The topsoil that you have removed can, of course, be used elsewhere in the garden wherever it is needed for flower beds or borders.

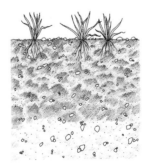

A fertile topsoil will encourage the growth of vigorous plants.

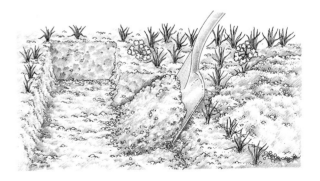

Removing the upper layer will get rid of the weed seeds and leave a less fertile soil, more suited to growing wild flowers.

Ox-eye daisy (Leucanthemum vulgare) and yarrow (Achillea millefolium) are two of the strongest growing wild flowers, able to compete well with vigorous grasses on fertile soils.

Using wood mulch Digging uncomposted wood or bark mulch, sawdust or newspaper into your soil will reduce its fertility levels for two to three years. When decomposition occurs, bacteria digest the carbon in organic matter and to do this they need nitrogen; the higher the carbon-to-nitrogen ratio in the organic matter, the more they will draw in nitrogen from the surrounding soil.

The gardener aims to have a high proportion of nitrogen in a compost heap so that it decomposes quickly. Wood products, with their high-carbon and low-nitrogen content, are the last thing they want, as they will rob the heap of nitrogen and, if put on the garden, will carry on robbing the soil of nitrogen for years. This, of course, is exactly what the wild flower gardener wants – nitrogen being locked up, so that it cannot feed greedy weed species and grasses.

Tough wild flowers for fertile soils

If you are reluctant to reduce the fertility of the rich loam that constitutes your garden soil, you could limit yourself to those vigorous wild flowers (listed in the panel on the right) that can fight off the weeds and other unwanted strong growers. Equally, it might be difficult to get wild flowers going in certain parts of the garden, such as awkward corners or steep banks that make working on or maintenance an impossible task or a hazardous one. Or you might have a patch that, however hard you try, always gets overrun by rough grass, but you can overcome this by sticking to the vigorous wild flowers that will cope with such situations. They are often the ones that you do not want to have too much of elsewhere in the wild flower garden. But though they may lack delicacy, they are not dull, and will do a first-class job in bringing colour to the garden in full summer. The plants listed are the toughest and most robust wild flowers, but any others that you see described as 'invasive' or 'impossible to eradicate' can also be useful in these situations.

This sort of planting will need only the occasional trim, perhaps once a year in the autumn, but more frequently if there is competition from weeds. The tough stems of many of the plants listed could damage a motor mower, so you will need to use a scythe or a strimmer (see page 86).

TOUGH WILD FLOWERS
Achillea millefolium
Adaptable, summer-flowering (white); H and S 30–60cm (1–2ft).
Daucus carota
Summer-flowering (white) and seeds itself vigorously; H 45–60cm (1½–2ft); S 30cm (1ft).
Eupatorium fistulosum
Intimidates weeds through its sheer size; late summer-flowering (pale pink); H 2m (6½ft); S 45cm (1½ft).
Geranium 'Claridge Druce'
Flowers at mid-summer (bright pink); H 60cm (2ft); S 90cm (3ft).
Leucanthemum vulgare
A mass of yellow-centred white flowers at mid-summer; spreads well; H 45–90cm (1½–3ft); S 60–90cm (2–3ft).
Prunella vulgaris
Summer-flowering (purple); H and S 20–30cm (8–12in).
Saponaria officinalis
Beautiful, pale pink flowers in summer; strongly spreading; H and S 1m (3ft 3in).
Solidago species
Vigorous growers, useful for late summer colour (yellow); H 90cm–2m (3–6½ft); S 90cm (3ft).
Tanacetum vulgare
Pretty yellow button flowers in summer; H 90cm–2m (3–6½ft); S 90cm (3ft).

Creating a meadow

Where there is a large expanse of ground to cover, the easiest and certainly the cheapest way of creating a wild flower meadow is to sow a seed mix directly into the ground. With smaller areas it becomes more practicable to consider planting (see page 82), or a mixture of sowing and planting. A problem with sowing is the time taken until you see the results, many wild flowers being slow to germinate and then to reach flowering size. This time-lag also means that the more vigorous species may end up dominating the plant community. Many gardeners may want to consider sowing the bulk of their wild flowers and grasses but planting out areas of greatest visibility.

Wild flower seed mixtures

It is now possible to buy what amounts to a meadow in a packet – a collection of grass and wild flower species, mixed and ready to sow. This can create the illusion that making a wild flower meadow is as easy as making a lawn – but it will take considerably longer to establish and there then is more scope for things to go wrong.

When buying wild flower mixes, look carefully at the ingredients. Some meadow mixes on sale are really only 'nine-day wonders', with an emphasis on fast-growing, cheap and cheerful annuals such as

A LATE SPRING MEADOW

1 *Cardamine pratensis* (lady's smock)
2 *Bellis perennis* (daisy)
3 *Fritillaria meleagris* (snake's-head fritillary)
4 *Hyacinthoides non-scripta* (bluebell)
5 *Lamium galeobdolon* (yellow archangel)
6 *Lamium album* (white dead-nettle)

7 *Lychnis flos-cuculi* (ragged robin)
8 *Primula veris* (cowslip)
9 *Ranunculus acris* (meadow buttercup)
10 *Silene dioica* (red campion)
11 *Stellaria holostea* and *S. graminea* (stitchwort)
12 *Taraxacum officinale* (dandelion)

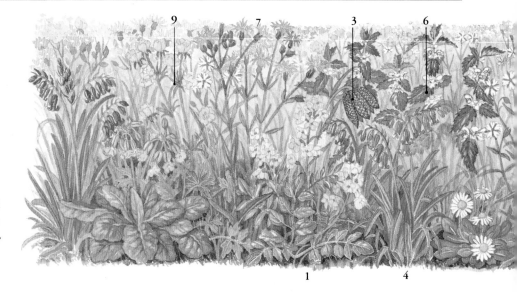

LEFT *An incredibly bright selection of cornfield wild flowers – mauve* corncockle (Agrostemma githago)*, red poppy* (Papaver rhoeas)*, yellow corn marigold* (Chrysanthemum segetum)*, and blue cornflower* (Centaurea cyanus)*. Growing at this density and in this combination they are quite unlike anything in nature but make a most attractive and easy-to-establish garden feature.*

poppies (*Papaver rhoeas*). These can be fine for some purposes, but they will not provide enough sound perennial plants for colour beyond the first season, or as the basis for a stable plant community. Other seed mixes include rather too many robust growers, plants that can take over, pushing aside less vigorous species. There is certainly a place for these plants – fertile or wet soils, for instance, on which plants grow more lush than they do on poorer, drier soils, or 'difficult' areas, where only plants with muscle will survive – but they can be too much of a good thing. The best approach to buying wild flower seed mix is to take your time and do your homework. Send off for all the mail-order catalogues and look up the plants for each mix in a wild flower guide so that you know exactly what is being offered.

You may prefer to make your own mix, incorporating the wild flowers that you like, and which are appropriate for your soil and conditions or perhaps native to your locality. This is easily done by ordering seed of each species separately and sowing it with a suitable grass mix. For meadows and other open areas a proportion of 60–80 per cent (by weight) of grass, with the remainder made up of wild flower seed, works well. If you have only a small area to plant, you may want to have more colour – that is,

more flowers and less grass – in which case you can make up a mix with a higher proportion of wild flower seed, or even no grass at all. Most seed companies will advise on the amount of each species to use. A suitable grass mix should never include rye grass (*Lolium perenne*) or a large proportion of other strong-growing agricultural grasses like timothy (*Phleum pratense*) or cocksfoot (*Dactylis glomerata*).

If you find it difficult to buy wild flower seed that is typical of your region, you could always collect seed from the wild (see page 96), but this can be time-consuming. A better answer may lie in the hay. Freshly cut hay from a flower-rich meadow, certainly if it is cut when green and then loose-baled, will contain a quantity of seed from grasses and flowers. Simply scatter the hay over ground prepared for seed sowing (see page 78), firm it down, and leave it. As the hay decomposes, the seed will fall out and start to germinate. The results will not mirror the source field exactly, in that species with plentiful seed will be somewhat over-represented, but it will be a start. In some countries, like Britain, seed from meadows in nature reserves – places that are especially rich in a variety of wild flowers – is now commercially collected using specially designed harvesters and sold by major wild flower seed suppliers.

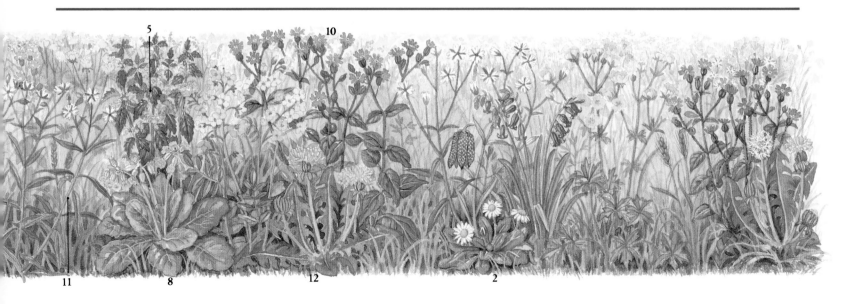

Sowing in the ground

Any kind of gardening is like painting a room, to the extent that most of the work lies in preparation rather than the actual painting. This is especially the case in preparing a suitable area for sowing, where you need to provide the best possible conditions for seed to germinate and develop and to minimize competition from weeds. Weed control (see page 72) is particularly important in areas which are going to be sown, since the weed roots will have a headstart on the growth of seed, and weed seeds usually grow faster than the seed of the wild flowers you want.

The best time to sow depends on your local climate. In cold-winter areas sowing should be done only in spring. In regions with hot, dry summers the ideal time is autumn as the seedlings can grow during the cooler winter months before having to face the summer droughts. Temperate, maritime climates have the most latitude in timing, both autumn and spring being suitable.

Vegetable growers will be familiar with the proverbial fine tilth that is best for seed germination. For wild flower gardening, you do not have to worry about getting it quite as fine as for vegetable growing, since on a large scale this would be both impractical and time-consuming. But the soil needs to be fairly well broken down to provide a good bed for seeds to germinate and for delicate seedlings to establish themselves. On a small scale the surface can be prepared with fork and rake, in the way that one would prepare the ground for sowing a lawn. On a larger scale, rotovating (see page 72) and rolling is necessary. Some growers recommend that for large areas the soil preparation should be quite shallow, rotovating only the top 5cm (2in). It is certainly easier to get a good fine tilth this way and fewer weed seeds will be brought up from below.

Broadcast sowing

Sowing seed evenly is not easy, and it might be best to have a practice first with sand. Divide your site into small, equally sized areas and then divide the seed into equal amounts, to ensure even distribution. Gardeners who are used to sowing lawns will have to adjust to sowing much more thinly. The sowing rate (the quantity of seed to be sown per unit area) varies with the kind of mix, and is generally given in the supplier's literature. As a general rule you should allow approximately 3–5g per square metre ($\frac{1}{8}$oz per square yard) for grass and flower mixtures and 1–2g ($\frac{1}{16}$oz) for flower seed only, where you are adding wild flowers to turf. The lie of the land can be exploited to choose the best site for species with particular requirements, such as wetland varieties like lady's smocks and ironweeds in hollows, or drought-tolerant ones such as wild carrot and wild marjoram on freely draining slopes.

Meadow buttercups (Ranunculus acris) and red campion (Silene dioica) are two wild flowers that are especially easy to grow from seed. They are growing alongside purslane (Claytonia sibirica), an annual wild flower of Asian origin that flourishes in damp places.

Broadcast sowing in drifts

You may broadcast the seed by hand, by walking up and down the site slowly, scattering seed as you walk, or with a wheeled seed sower. Mix the seed with sand to aid even distribution and to budget your seed for two sowings, the second made by walking at right angles to the tracks of your first. If you are sowing grasses and wild flowers separately, you can create interesting effects by sowing different species in drifts (see page 41). It may also be sensible to sow the more expensive species in small pockets.

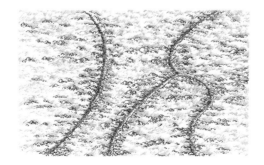

Divide the area to be sown roughly into patches, using the back of a rake or a spade.

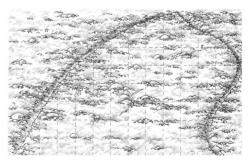

Walk across the site, making a second sowing of each species at right angles to the first.

Seed can be surface-sown with no covering, but since partial burial is beneficial to the germination of many species, some attempt should be made to cover the seed thinly. A small area can easily be raked over, which will have the effect of burying a proportion of seed a few millimetres down. Firming by light treading will also improve germination, as it will bring the seed into better contact with the soil. On a larger scale, raking can be carried out using a weighted sheet of wire mesh, dragged across the seedbed, to cover the seed; firming on this scale is best done with a roller, to improve germination.

Germination

The only immediate after-care required by sown areas is to try to keep the birds off; you want to encourage wildlife eventually, but not quite yet. After a week or two a slight haze of green will become apparent; this is the magic of germination, as thousands of seemingly dry little husks become alive, and develop into tiny wisps of green leaf. Germination of grasses, annuals and some perennials will be rapid, but other perennials will take their time. Many plants of northern climates need winter chilling before they germinate, so will not appear until the following spring – they have evolved in this way to delay growth until the days are warmer.

Nurse crops

This is a way of protecting perennial wild flower seedlings which, because they are often slow to establish, can leave a soil vulnerable to erosion. An annual crop is sown with the wild flower mix, which fills in the space for the first year. On poor soils an annual variety of rye grass can be used such as 'Westerwolds' rye grass, a form of *Lolium multiflorum*, but it must be cut before it seeds. It would be too strong-growing for fertile soils, however. In small gardens the best alternative is to mix some annuals in with the seed to provide a splash of colour for the first year. Next year the nurse crop will have all but disappeared, to be replaced by the first of the perennial wild flowers. Cornfield wild flowers or other small, light growing annuals that germinate quickly provide the ideal nurse crop for most situations (see page 86).

Sowing seed in furrows

Divide up the site and the seed into equal portions beforehand. Then make a series of furrows, or shallow 'trenches', with the back of a hoe or rake, about 1cm (½in) deep and 30cm (1ft) apart across the site. Scatter the seed thinly, fill the furrows by raking diagonally over them, then gently firm by walking heel to toe along each one. It will look incongruous at first, to have a meadow coming up in straight lines, but the plants will soon grow together and cover the bare ground in between.

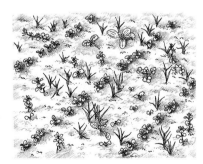

Weeds can easily be distinguished at this stage – and removed.

The mid-summer meadow

This is one of the most popular wild flower garden features, and deservedly so: it is somehow the encapsulation of the countryside in summer. It does not grow too tall, 30–45cm (1–1½ft), and so is suitable for most sizes of garden, although meadows always look best on a large scale. The plants shown here are appropriate for all well-drained soils; many will do well on dry and infertile soils too. Meadows are a rich habitat and a little research will reveal other suitable wild flowers for this time of year, including ox-eye daisy and yarrow.

1 *Stokesia laevis* (stoke's aster): 30–45cm (1–1½ft); often grown as a garden plant; likes moist, acid soils.

2 *Filipendula vulgaris* (dropwort): 45cm (1½ft); does best on light or limy soils.

3 *Heliopsis helianthoides* (ox-eye): 1.2–1.8m (4–6ft); a robust and adaptable plant; dislikes dry sites.

4 *Malva moschata* (musk mallow): 30–45cm (1–1½ft); a good bee plant; the mallow prefers light soils.

1 2 3 4 5 6 7 8

5 *Ranunculus acris* (buttercup): 20–30cm (8–12in); clump-forming perennial with golden yellow flowers.

6 *Geranium pratensis* (meadow cranesbill): 75–90cm (2½–3ft); can be very successful, but needs to be planted rather than sown.

7 *Centaurea scabiosa* (greater knapweed): 30–75cm (1–1½ft); spectacular grown *en masse*; a good butterfly plant.

8 *Galium verum* (lady's bedstraw): sprawls over 90cm (3ft); best on light soils.

9 *Trifolium pratense* (clover): 10–20cm (4–8in); summer flowers and attractive leaves.

10 *Hypericum perforatum* (st john's wort): 45–90cm (1½–3ft); has many traditional medicinal uses.

11 *Knautia arvensis* (field scabious): 30–90cm (1–3ft); a good butterfly plant.

12 *Polemonium caeruleum* (jacob's ladder): 60–75cm (2–2½ft); easy to establish and spreads well.

13 *Coreopsis lanceolata* (lance-leaved coreopsis):

30–60cm (1–2ft); robust and spreads easily.

14 *Scabiosa columbaria* (small scabious): 30–45cm (1–1½ft); flowers over a long period; prefers light soils.

15 *Rhinanthus major* (yellow rattle): 20–30cm (8–12in); an annual semi-parasite that needs to be sown in autumn with grasses, but easily establishes itself.

16 *Vicia cracca* (tufted vetch): stems scramble to 2m (6½ft) long, hanging onto other plants for support.

9   11   12   13   14   15   16

10

Planting in grass

Planting gives the gardener greater certainty and quicker results, although it is more expensive and time-consuming. In an existing meadow or area of grass, seed may not stand much of a chance, and in a new meadow, planting out some perennials will give a year's headstart over seed. In any case, some wild flower species may well be difficult to obtain as seed.

New sites need to be as weed-free as possible and should preferably be dug over or rotovated to facilitate root penetration. You should also be able to plant in an area of low grass, such as a wild flower lawn, without too much competition from the existing plants. But planting into dense vegetation such as a thriving meadow means putting a new plant into a situation where it must face a lot of competition. The ground around the newcomer needs to be cleared first, to prevent weed seeds being brought up to the surface and starting to grow. Prepare each planting site first by using one of the methods for killing weeds (see page 73) to clear a small space. Several weeks later the grass will be dead and you will be ready to plant.

Work a volume of soil wider and deeper than the plant's rootball by turning it over with a fork, before inserting the plant. On poor, thin soils, add some bonemeal to the bottom of the planting hole, and in dry weather fill the hole with water before planting.

The depth of planting should be equivalent to what it was before. If you needed to remove dead turf in order to prepare the planting hole, make sure that it goes back the way it was so that buried weed seeds remain underground. The dead turf may not look pretty, but it is better than having thistles or docks suffocating the new plants, and in a few months the turf will have grown in again from the sides.

Some herbaceous plants in grass are easily damaged by having a mower driven over them, notably those, such as columbines (*Aquilegia*), with a single bud or shoot sticking up above ground level. Put them into a slight hollow, so that the base of the plant is below the level of the grass, and therefore protected from bearing the full weight of the mower.

Planting out seedlings you have raised yourself offers a compromise between sowing and planting a meadow. It is possible to sow a meadow mix in pots or trays, then plant out clumps of young plants comprising grasses and wild flowers. This at least lets them steal a march on the plants you do not want and allows you to hoe out weed seedlings between the clumps in the first year. By the second year the level of weed seed in the top layer of soil should be reduced and the clumps will start to spread out.

A variation on this technique is to sow in trays the more valuable seed mix that contains the wild flowers, plant them out as seedlings, and fill in the intervening spaces with a grass seed mix. Starting off seed in

A WILD FLOWER LAWN

1 *Bellis perennis* (daisy)
2 *Hypochaeris radicata* (cat's ear)
3 *Lotus corniculatus* (bird's foot trefoil)
4 *Prunella vulgaris* (self-heal)
5 *Trifolium pratense* (clover)
6 *Veronica chamaedrys* (germander speedwell)

5   4   1   3   2   6

Prunella vulgaris
Self-heal is a small but robust and quickly spreading perennial wild flower that thrives in sun or part-shade and survives well among vigorous grasses in a meadow. As its name indicates, it was once used in herbal medicine, especially for treating wounds and sore throats. It is popular with a wide range of insects, especially since it flowers after the majority of early-summer wild flowers.

Cornflow
cyanus) a
(Papaver
colourful
sowing e
are not to
grasses a
perennia
done bot
several ti
provide a
flowers.

trays is especially useful on heavy clay soils, where it is impossible to break the soil up sufficiently to be able to sow seed directly in the ground. For larger-scale sowings, it is more appropriate to make and plant out your own wild flower turves (see below).

When to plant
The form in which wild flowers are planted will determine the best time of year to plant them out.

Bare-rooted plants In cool, moist climates, almost any time of year between late summer and late spring is fine for digging up herbaceous plants and transplanting them. In hotter climates it is best done in autumn or early winter, so that roots can grow and establish before the summer. In areas with a long, hard winter, plant as soon as possible after the ice in the soil has melted.

Container-grown plants Using plants grown in containers minimizes root damage when planting out and gives the gardener greater flexibility in planting time. In temperate climates, they can be planted at any time of year, provided they are kept watered. But in continental climates, with hard winters, planting should be left until spring.

Seedlings Young plants raised in seed trays (see page 98) need to be put out at a time of year when they run no risk of drying out or being frozen. In cold climates this means spring, and in warm ones, where frost is unlikely, autumn or winter.

Creating a wild flower lawn
The wild flower lawn is particularly useful for those places where a full-blown meadow is too tall or too informal. It consists of standard lawn grass with a population of wild flowers that will happily grow and flower at only a little more than normal lawn height. The easiest way to start is simply to stop mowing for a while and see what comes up. The chances are that there will be a fair number of wild flowers in it to start with, plants like daisies, clovers and plantains that have ground-hugging rosettes and short flower stalks. There may also be self-heal if you are lucky, as well as larger wild flowers like yarrow that can survive being constantly cropped by the mower, but never have the chance to flower.

It is now possible to buy ready-mixed wild flower lawn seed but if you want to enrich an existing lawn, seeds or plants can be inserted by 'scarification' (see below). The most suitable wild flowers for a lawn are late spring to summer flowerers, but there are some earlier ones, notably the cowslip and in shadier patches even the primrose if you do not cut too short. Another possibility for the spring are small bulbs like snowdrops, crocuses and the smaller *Narcissus* species. For maintenance of the lawn, see page 86.

Wild flower turf

Wild flower turf or sod can be used to create or to enrich a lawn or meadow. Sow a wild flower and grass seed mix into a prepared, weed-free seedbed, sowing a little more densely than usual. Leave it to grow for several months, over the summer, until it forms a solid mat of young plants. Then dig it up, slicing at a depth of 5–8cm (2–3in) below the surface with a spade, to form rectangular turves. Use them to plant out a meadow area, placing them in shallow depressions in the ground.

If you leave more than 30cm (1ft) between turves, sow some more grass seed in between.

Use a sturdy rake to tear through patches of lawn or meadow, to expose bare earth. These can be planted or sown with wild flower seed, to enrich it or to introduce a species in drifts. Firm the soil afterwards.

Cre

Althou
meado
small-s
garden
meado
reliabl
wild fl
short.
beautif
extrem
ing pe
in the
and otl

Sowir
Autun
soil is
in pat
outline
stones
rapidly
after tl

Early :
weeds
anothe
a sligh

Maintaining meadows

Any wild flower planting will change over time, but meadows perhaps more than most. Some species will germinate and develop rapidly, giving a good show in the second year after sowing, such as yarrow and self-heal, whereas others, like cowslips, will take longer. The proportion of species, and therefore the appearance of the meadow, will change as the plant community settles down to something approaching an equilibrium. It may take several years until the meadow reaches a point at which the species in it are mature and more or less in balance, none making extensive growth at the expense of others. But to maintain this balance you will have to follow a rigorous maintenance regime.

We have already seen that the existence of agricultural meadows depends on cutting, mowing or grazing (see page 44). As a gardener, you will have to apply these controlling factors to your meadow, to keep at bay the vegetation that threatens to turn them into something else. The immediate threat is not from trees or even scrub taking over, but coarse weedy grasses and perennials. Even the wild flowers themselves have to be kept in some kind of balance.

In the garden, the balance of wild flower species is dependent on your programme of cutting. The timing of cutting is different for spring and summer meadows. A spring-flowering meadow, with cow-

slips and buttercups for example, would need to be cut in mid-summer, well after the flowering season, giving the wild flowers enough time to seed. Leaving it longer than this could mean that grasses and any larger summer-flowering species like knapweeds will grow too tall and crowd out the spring flowers.

Unless there are spring flowers like bulbs and cowslips, a wild flower lawn should be cut to around 5cm (2in) until late spring, when it should be left uncut for about a month, as this will be its main flowering season. Thereafter it should be cut every two to four weeks, to 8–10cm (3–4in), which will allow for some further flowering. If there *are* early spring flowers, leave the first cut of the year until the bulb leaves have yellowed.

Self-seeding

In nature, wild flowers are continually renewing themselves, either through self-seeding or by runners. Some plants, such as the pasque flower, will go on for years and years in the same patch, but many wild flowers and grasses are continually swapping places; bergamot, for instance, constantly grows outwards from the centre of its original starting place. With many species, the younger individuals are more vigorous; they grow faster and flower better. It is therefore in the gardener's interest to encourage self-seeding. The danger is that one species may begin to take over, but it should be

AN A

Light g
planted
1 *Agro*
(cornco
2 *Antl*
(corn c
3 *Cen*
(cornflo
4 *Chr*
segetu
5 *Pap*
(comm

A CHALK DOWNLAND

1 *Campanula glomerata* (clustered bellflower)
2 *Campanula rotundifolia* (harebell, scottish bluebell)
3 *Centaurea nigra* (lesser knapweed)
4 *Dianthus gratianopolitanus* (cheddar pink)
5 *Helianthemum nummularium*

(common rock rose)
6 *Linaria vulgaris* (toadflax)
7 *Linum perenne* (flax)
8 *Origanum vulgare* (marjoram)
9 *Reseda lutea* (wild mignonette)
10 *Salvia pratensis* (meadow clary)
11 *Sanguisorba minor* (salad burnet)

12 *Thymus praecox* (wild thyme)

Lilium martagon
*The pink flowers of the
martagon lily have a turk's
cap form, with recurving
petals, hence its other
common name. This majestic
summer-flowering bulb needs
time and patience to
establish on any scale but its
distinctive beauty makes it
well worth the effort. Its
seeds take two years to
germinate, the root emerging
the first spring after sowing
and the shoot the next. It
will then take several more
years to produce flowers, but
its saving grace is that, once
established, it produces a
quantity of seeds.*

possible to discourage this species by preventing it from self-seeding. On a small scale, this can be done by individual cutting, but on a larger scale the whole meadow would need to be cut before the invasive species sets seed. If one or two species still threaten to become too dominant, you may have to resort to 'spot-weeding' techniques (see page 73).

In a wild flower lawn, if certain wild flowers, such as daisies and self-heal, start to predominate over the grass, you should reduce their numbers by digging up a proportion and replacing them with strips of turf, or sowing grass seed in the bare patches. On the whole though, a regular cutting programme will ensure that no one species becomes dominant.

Mowing meadows

Many ordinary mowers are designed to cut only lawns, not wild flower meadows. Cylinder mowers and hover mowers cut far too short, and some rotary mowers are impossible to set high enough. A full-blown summer meadow will need cutting with a mower where the blades can be set at their highest, a minimum of 7cm (2¾in), while areas such as wild flower lawns or spring meadows that are to be kept as lawns through the summer can be cut lower, to 5cm (2in). Many spring wild flowers are either bulbs that will disappear underground or they have flat rosettes of foliage that can survive being cut as low as lawn grasses. Larger perennials in meadows can be dam-

aged by heavy machines, notably ride-on mowers where your own weight is added to the mower's.

It may prove impossible to cut tall meadows with a mower, and the best unmechanized approach is with a scythe. Once you have learnt to use a scythe, from somebody who is accustomed to using one, it can be a wonderfully therapeutic experience, rhythmically swinging and swishing your way through the grass. You should always wear good foot protection when using a scythe. For those who are determined to be part of the twentieth century, the mechanized alternative is the strimmer. For grass and light plant material, the nylon flail of the strimmer can be used, but if it keeps snapping this means that the vegetation is too tough, and you will have to fit the blade. A strimmer is even more dangerous than a scythe, and you should wear goggles, trousers of strong material and sturdy footwear, as bits of stalk and stones are sent flying in all directions. After an hour or so, you may feel that you want some ear protection as well: strimming is noisy and, unlike scything, it is not therapeutic.

Unless the soil is very infertile, it is advisable to remove clippings, to help to keep fertility low and thereby help less vigorous species. Raking up cuttings is a rather tedious activity so if you are using a mower, one with a grass box is an advantage. You should never feed a wild flower lawn with lawn food, as the best results are to be had on poorer soils.

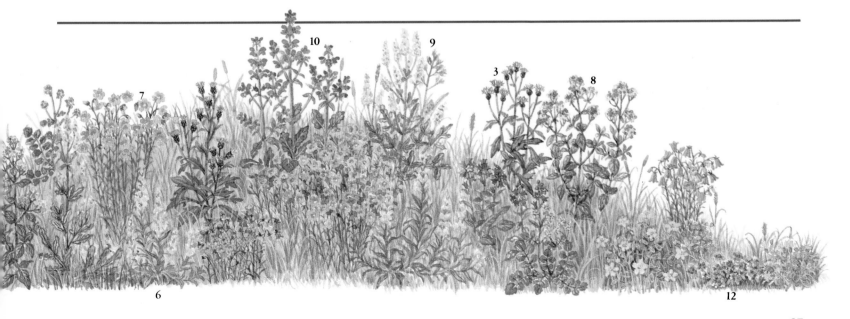

Planting in shade

Wild flower gardens in shade will on the whole have to be planted, as many woodland species are very slow to grow from seed: trilliums and many lilies, for instance, take two years to come up, and several more to flower. Certain choice woodland wild flowers, such as the two just mentioned, are slow to propagate by any means, and consequently have suffered considerably from the depredations of commercial wild flower collection. However, a good many woodland wild flowers can be easily and cheaply obtained as plants, like solomon's seal (*Polygonatum* and *Smilacina*), and lily-of-the-valley (*Convallaria majalis*). These can be planted extensively, with fewer of the rare and expensive plants like trilliums put in special places, where they can be given extra attention and be easily seen. Some woodlanders do seed easily and give quick results, but there are far fewer of them than for sunnier habitats; primroses and violets are two good examples. Many woodland plants, especially spring-flowering ones, are bulbs and these should be planted as early in the autumn as possible, since their roots start growing as soon as they are in the ground (see below). Plant bulbs in drifts by throwing them down in handfuls to help create a random, more natural effect (see page 41).

Woodland plants live in a very different kind of soil to that of meadows and open country. The upper layer is composed of undecayed leaves, beneath which there is a layer of soft, humus-rich material, known as leafmould. The roots of woodland plants are quite shallow, running around near the surface in the damp and rich leafmould. If you are planting shade-loving wild flowers in a wood you should have no problems, but if you are planting underneath isolated trees in gardens there may not be a decent layer of leafmould underneath, nor will you find any in artificially created shady places. For woodland plants to succeed in these situations, it is necessary to build up a layer of organic matter in the soil with imported material such as composted bark, mushroom compost (although this contains lime), well-rotted garden compost or decayed leaves. On dry sites it might be worth considering adding 'hydrogel': a recently invented soil additive that increases the water-holding capacity of the soil; directions on the container should be followed as to the quantity to use. Considerable quantities of the compost material need to be dug in thoroughly, to incorporate them into the top spit of soil before planting.

If the shaded area in your garden is more or less natural woodland, you may need to thin out some of the vegetation (bear in mind that many localities

Planting bulbs

Once you have decided on the rough outline of their planting, scatter the bulbs by gently throwing a handful on the ground, and then plant them where they land. Bury the bulbs at a depth equivalent to twice their height; firm them in well after planting, with gentle pressure from the feet, so that good contact is made with the soil. Various bulb planting tools have been invented, although in my experience they are not a great improvement on a trowel and spade, and they can be almost useless on heavy soils.

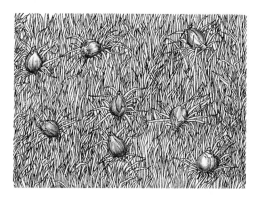

Plant the bulbs where they land to help create a random, more natural effect.

The general rule with bulb planting is to plant them at twice their height.

Trillium sessile *is one of several woodland wild flowers that are slow and difficult to propagate, taking two years to germinate from seed. Like other such species, its wild populations have suffered from commercial collecting.*

Applying a mulch

Once you have planted your woodland wild flowers, you need to put a generous quantity of mulch around them straight away, to suppress weeds and to keep their roots cool and moist (see below).

There are several different types of mulch, including straw, spent hops and mushroom compost, and you should use whatever waste product is available locally. Bark mulch and wood chips are a waste product from the forestry industry, now widely used in gardens. They can be expensive to buy in any quantity, although if you have waste wood or prunings you could make your own with a shredder. Uncomposted conifer wood and bark should be used cautiously around herbaceous plants though, as it releases toxins which can burn tender young growth. The key is to use it around the crowns of plants, rather than covering them.

As we saw in the section on Soil fertility, page 74, wood and bark chippings can be used to reduce the level of nitrogen available to plants if they are dug into the soil. (This also applies to straw but to a lesser extent.) However, in woodland situations this is not usually desired, so care needs to be taken to ensure that they are not incorporated into the soil during planting and other gardening operations.

have restrictions on tree removal) for your wild flower planting. Some shrubs and other undergrowth will probably need to be taken out, but otherwise the soil should need little amendment beyond the removal of smaller tree roots and any undesired plants, since vigorous weedy species are not a great problem in woodlands. The chances are that there will be some desirable wild flowers in place already, in which case the role of the wild flower gardener is to work round them as far as possible.

Mulching

The use of a mulch between plants conserves moisture and suppresses the growth of weed seedlings, creating something like the top layer of loose leaf litter found in woodland soils. Woodland or shade plantings are done more thinly than full sunlight ones, so a covering to stop weeds is important. Straw makes an excellent mulch: it is cheap, easy to obtain, and apply and lasts for two seasons. Apart from the odd 'volunteer' of wheat or barley and a tendency to harbour slugs, it has much to recommend it.

Once you have planted your woodland wild flowers, a generous quantity of mulch needs to be put around them, to keep their roots cool and moist.

Planting plan for a late spring woodland

Some of the finest early wild flower sights are to be found in woodlands, where the ground is covered in a rich variety of different species, flowering before the trees have grown their leaves. Many of these wild flowers will spread quite quickly, like primroses, violets and creeping phlox, while others, especially trilliums and bloodroots, are very slow. These slow species need to be planted where you can see them to best advantage, with the quicker-growing ones scattered around to grow into natural-looking drifts. A spongy, humus-rich soil is needed for success, so be generous with compost or other organic matter.

1   2   3   4   5   6   7   8   9   10   11

1 *Aquilegia canadensis* (columbine): 75cm (2½ft); colourful and spreads easily.

2 *Galium odoratum* (woodruff): 15cm (6in); spreads and thrives in dry shade; prefers lime.

3 *Primula elatior* (oxlip): 25cm (10in); likes moist soil.

4 *Phlox stolonifera* (creeping phlox): 20cm (8in); one of the most colourful ground covers for light shade and acid soils.

5 *Thelypteris hexagonopetra* (broad beech fern): 40cm (16in); one of the best ground covers.

6 *Erythronium umbilicatum* (trout lily): 20cm (8in); slowly spreads; prefers rich, moist soil.

7 *Trillium grandiflorum* (wake robin): 40cm (16in); a classic woodlander, liking acid soil.

8 *Polystichum acrostichoides* (christmas fern): 30–60cm (1–2ft); a tough evergreen fern.

9 *Sanguinaria canadensis* (bloodroot): 10cm (4in); brief spring flowers but attractive leaves all summer; needs rich soil.

10 *Helleborus foetidus* (hellebore): 60–90cm (2–3ft); stately evergreen; prefers lime.

11 *Viola riviniana* (dog violet): 10cm (4in); very early flowering; does well on moist soil.

12 *Convallaria majalis* (lily-of-the-valley): 15cm (6in); sweetly scented; a strong-growing spreader.

13 *Primula vulgaris* (primrose): 15cm (6in); easy and adaptable classic spring wild flower.

14 *Dryopteris filix-mas* (male fern): to 90cm (3ft); sometimes evergreen, adaptable fern.

15 *Dicentra eximia* (wild bleeding heart): 30cm (1ft); flowers for ages, spreading well.

16 *Anemone nemorosa* (wood anemone): 15cm (6in); a steady spreader on poor soils.

17 *Chrysogonum virginianum* (green and gold): 20cm (8in); excellent ground cover for light shade; long flowering season.

18 *Silene virginica* (fire-pink): 30–60cm (1–2ft); does best in only light shade.

19 *Mertensia virginica* (virginia bluebell): 40–60cm (16in–2ft); does well on moist rich soils; dies back in summer.

12   13   14   15   16   17   18   19

Creating and planting wetlands

If you have a naturally damp or waterlogged area in your garden, this is the obvious place to enhance with moisture-loving wild flowers. Alternatively, a small pond and wetland area can be created on dry land by using pond lining materials (see below). Their value as garden features and oases for wildlife make them well worth the trouble of building, especially as they are usually very quick to establish and immensely rewarding. And wetland areas require little maintenance, except for an annual cut in the autumn or winter to remove dead stems.

A natural area of damp ground is easy enough to plant, but first it has to be cleared and any unwanted vegetation will be dense, with matted root systems. Digging wet ground is always hard work, especially if there is a layer of clay. Weedkillers can be used to clear grass and weeds, but care should be taken when using them near water, especially running water. Chemicals that are normally safe to use, like glyphosate, depend on being absorbed by soil particles and then broken down by bacteria. They will not be absorbed in the same way in water, and will remain active for considerably longer, with possible lethal results for water life.

One of the keys to an interesting and lively wetland area is to provide a diversity of 'micro-habitats' by varying the levels, and hence the moisture content, of the ground. If the water table is consistently close to ground level over a substantial area, then you may want to excavate part of it to create a pond. Over areas of slightly wet ground small patches can be lowered and others raised so that the moisture needs of a wide variety of plants, from marshland wild flowers to marginal plants like water irises, can be provided for.

It is often easier to plant wetlands or moist meadows rather than sow them, especially if there is a risk that running water will wash seeds away. Planting can be done at any time (see page 82), although spring would provide the best combination of pleasant working conditions and moist soil. Permanently moist ground is a boon to weeds, so mulching between plants is a help (see page 89). If you have a large area to plant, however, it may be worth sowing some seeds, perhaps planting more expensive or slower-growing kinds of wild flower. Or you could plant out the flowering and ornamental species and sow a seed mixture of moisture-loving grasses around them (see page 76).

The banks of streams and rivers are among the most beautiful wild flower habitats when they are mature, but they can be difficult sites to work on.

Making a marsh

Marshes have poor drainage but they are never naturally stagnant, so your aim is to create limited drainage. Using thick plastic sheeting, punch holes in it, about 45cm (1½ft) apart, then bury the sheet at least 30cm (1ft) deep. The soil infill must be completely weed-free; if it is on the poor side, add some organic matter to enrich it. There are purpose-made trickle hoses designed for flower borders and lawns, or you can make your own with a piece of old hose, punching holes along its length with a nail.

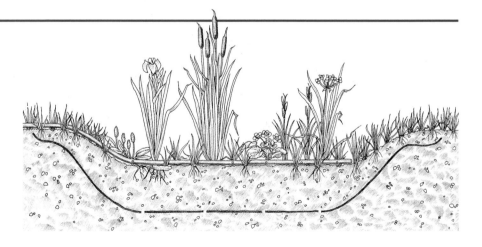

A length of trickle hose concealed around the marsh area will enable you to keep it moist in dry spells.

Many wetland wild flowers grow and spread vigorously after planting. The yellow monkey flower (Mimulus luteus) *seeds itself around, sometimes even to nuisance proportions, while the blue flag* (Iris versicolor) *spreads only slowly by seed, but soon forms solid clumps as its roots spread outwards.*

The steepness of the banks, the density of the weeds, the coldness of the water as well as the mud and the tree roots, all conspire to make bank planting hard work. The best idea might be to transplant some well-established plants among the vegetation already there and hope that they take. Vigorous growers such as purple loosestrifes (*Lythrum*), hemp agrimonies (*Eupatorium cannabinum*), and meadowsweets (*Filipendula ulmaria*) should establish themselves reasonably well. Spring is the best time of year to work on banks, so that the plants take root before the winter, and before the seasonal risk of flooding.

Making a wetland area on dry land

This may sound rather like one of the nature-defying practices that wild flower gardening is trying to get away from, but it is one that can be justified by the benefit it brings to a wide variety of wildlife. Many people would like to have a pond in the garden, to grow the wild flowers that are associated with water, and a pond will look much more natural if there is a neighbouring wetland area. A garden pond is generally made by creating an impervious layer with clay, cement or with a liner made from plastic sheeting or butyl rubber, so that water cannot run away. A wetland area next to the pond can be made by simply extending the impervious layer outwards at a shallower depth, and filling it with soil. But since it is not necessary to have a totally impervious layer below a wetland, it may be better (and is certainly cheaper) to make the marsh area separately (see opposite, below).

Planting plan for wetland wild flowers

The margins of a pond or an area of wet ground offer the wild flower gardener many exciting possibilities, with the lush growth of reeds, sedges and the often colourful wild flowers of these places. Marginal plants are those, like the yellow flag iris (*Iris pseudacorus*), that grow out of the water itself, although they can usually be grown in damp ground as well. Permanently moist soil supports a different cast of wild flowers, most of them summer-flowering. This wetland is shown in mid-summer.

Marshy meadow area:

1 *Polygonum bistorta* (bistort): 75cm (2½ft); summer-flowering; forms a clump rapidly.

2 *Hibiscus moscheutos* (rose mallow): 90–120cm (3–4ft); late summer-flowering; needs full sun.

3 *Mentha aquatica* (watermint): 45cm (1½ft); summer-flowering; vigorous, spreading quickly.

4 *Lythrum salicaria* (purple loosestrife): 60–120cm (2–4ft); summer-flowering; vigorous.

5 *Iris versicolor* (blue flag): 60–90cm (2–3ft); early summer-flowering.

6 *Filipendula ulmaria* (meadowsweet): 75–120cm (2½–4ft); superb summer wild flower for planting in drifts; scented.

7 *Lobelia cardinalis* (cardinal flower): 75–90cm (2½–3ft); late summer-flowering.

8 *Eupatorium cannabinum* (hemp agrimony): 75–120cm (2½–4ft): late summer-flowering.

9 *Stachys palustris* (marsh woundwort): 75cm (2½ft); mid-summer-flowering.

10 *Trollius laxus* (globeflower): 30–45cm (1–1½ft); mid-summer-flowering; likes sun.

11 *Osmunda regalis* (royal fern): 60–120cm (2–4ft); majestic fern for acid soils in full sun.

Marginal plants by pond side:

12 *Saururus cernuus* (lizard's tail): 60–90cm (2–3ft); summer-flowering; shade tolerant; a rapid spreader.

13 *Menyanthes trifoliata* (bogbean): 30cm (1ft); early spring-flowering.

14 *Iris pseudacorus* (yellow flag): 75cm–1.5m (2½–5ft); early summer-flowering; vigorous.

15 *Butomus umbellatus* (flowering rush): 75cm–1.5m (2½–5ft); summer-flowering.

16 *Ranunculus lingua* (greater spearwort): 90cm (3ft); summer-flowering; vigorous.

Propagation

Propagation is the art of increasing plants, of starting with a few and ending with many. This is of particular interest to wild flower gardeners, as a large number of plants of one species are often required. Planting, rather than sowing seed, for any reasonably sized area can be prohibitively expensive, but propagating one's own plants can reduce the cost of planting an area considerably.

Raising plants from seed is usually the quickest and easiest means of propagating large numbers of herbaceous wild flowers and grasses, but not woody plants like shrubs and trees which are very slow from seed. Seed-grown plants always show some degree of variation, and so seed is not generally suitable when you want to propagate a particular species or cultivar or a selection whose characteristics you want to preserve. For example, if you had an especially good, pale pink wood anemone (*Anemone nemorosa*), a very variable wild flower, it would have to be propagated by dividing the tubers, rather than by sowing seed, to preserve its best characteristics.

Seed-raised plants are always genetically mixed and therefore do not always exactly resemble their parents. To get plants that are identical to their parents, vegetative propagation is therefore needed – in other words, division or cuttings.

Seed collection

Seed might be collected from wild flowers already in the garden or from those growing wild. This fascinating business is not always easy, as seed is designed by nature for dispersal, not for neat collection. You will find yourself learning the quirks of every individual species, becoming adept at selecting the crucial moment when the seed is ripe, but still in place on the plant. Seed, being rich in protein, is a popular food with small birds and mammals so you may find that you are sometimes beaten to it. In my experience seedheads are also frequently infested with small insect larvae taking their share of the bounty, and it is vital for the rest of your harvest that they are not collected too. Different kinds of seed have varying characteristics and are best dealt with by a variety of means (see below).

Sorting the seed

Once seed is collected it should be stored in paper bags in a dry place for several days, primarily to dry it off, but in the case of seed in capsules, so that it can be released and fall to the bottom of the bag. Once dry, it can be cleaned and sorted. Separating seed from chaff is a process that can vary between the

Collecting seed

The various seed dispersal mechanisms used by plants are designed to scatter seed over distances, so you will need to be well aware of when the seed is ripening in order to have a good harvest. Shown on the right are examples of the more common types of seedhead to be found among wild flowers and the best method for collecting them in each case. Use paper bags or large envelopes to collect the seeds.

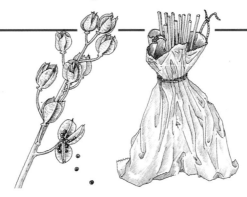

Capsule-like seedheads, common among foxgloves, bluebells and campions, are best collected by cutting off bunches before they open. Place them upside down in paper bags in a cool, dry place to release their seeds.

Seed with hair attached, designed to float away on the breeze, like that of members of the daisy family (Compositae), or bare seed held in heads, like the cow parsley family (Umbelliferae), can simply be pulled off and put straight into a paper bag.

Wild flower fruits come in all shapes and sizes, designed to distribute the seed they contain. Collecting the seed will involve getting to know the peculiarities of each species – when the seed is ripe, how easily it is extracted from the fruit and how it is best cleaned and separated from the chaff. Seed collection is a deeply satisfying business, although at times it can also be a frustrating one.

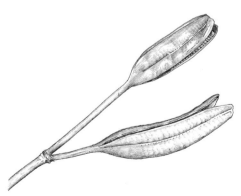

Some wild flowers, like irises and lilies, have large seeds which can only be extracted by breaking open the sides of the capsule.

Spring-loaded seedheads (like cranesbills), primed to explode over long distances, need to be picked off one by one; many will shoot off as you comb the plant. You might prefer to tie a paper bag over the seedheads before they explode.

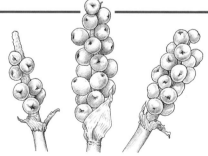

Some of the few herbaceous berrying plants are doll's eyes (Actaea) and arums. Berries are easily picked, and the seeds should be extracted quickly while the flesh is still soft. If you cannot deal with them straight away, dry them and store in a cool, dry place.

simple and the immensely frustrating – it is a process of trial, error and invention. However, for small-scale use, it does not have to be scrupulously clean. Coarse and fine-mesh sieves can be used for different seed, and you can also experiment with gently blowing away the chaff, but this works only with seeds that are relatively heavy in relation to their chaff. I find that most of the chaff can often be removed by passing a straight edge, such as a ruler, over a handful of seed scattered across a piece of paper laid on a flat surface.

Removing seed from berries is the most difficult job in my experience. Larger seeds can be extracted with sharp fingernails, while others are best dealt with by macerating the berries in a small quantity of water to soften them, and then separating the flesh from the seeds on a plate, using a knife. You will have to use your imagination and experiment with a variety of kitchen implements, but bear in mind that some berries (*Actaea* and *Arum*, for instance) are poisonous, so you should wash your hands and the implements thoroughly afterwards. It is worth going to some trouble to clean and wash berry-borne seed well, as the flesh of the berries sometimes contains germination inhibitors.

Seed that is not going to be sown straight away should be stored in cool, dry conditions. If it is to be kept in an airtight container it is essential that it is completely dry before being stored, otherwise it will rapidly become mouldy. The ideal solution is to keep seed in an airtight container with some silica gel, to absorb moisture and to store it in a domestic fridge, at a few degrees above 0°C (32°F).

Sowing wild flower seed

It is usually best to sow seed collected in the wild as soon as it is ripe and it should be sown in trays as described below. Although poppy seed may last for a hundred years, that is exceptional, and others, like milkweeds (*Asclepias*), will last for only a few months. Unlike the seed of cultivated flowers and vegetables that generally come up quickly and all at once, wild flowers can be different. It is not in the interests of a wild plant for all its seeds to germinate at once, as one late frost or a grazing rabbit could destroy all the seedlings in one go. As well as coming up sporadically, many plants will only germinate after the winter months, a sensible mechanism which ensures that particularly delicate seedlings do not have to risk a spell of cold weather.

Most herbaceous wild flowers germinate fairly well, and in fact most do not need the cold spell to make them come up, so they can be sown in the spring. Those that do need frost exposure are often related, making it possible to predict which will need sowing in the autumn. The following families have many members that need cold treatment: iris

Stratification

In this process, seed is chilled before it will germinate. Sow the seeds in trays as normal, then place each tray in a sealed plastic bag (to keep out rodents) and put it in a shaded spot outside during the winter months. Alternatively, seed can be mixed with damp sand and chilled in a refrigerator for a month. Keep it at a temperature of between 0–4°C (32–40°F), not below freezing which could damage the seed. This method is useful for seed that has been bought in the spring from a seed supplier.

When the weather warms up, check the trays every week, and remove the plastic bag once the seeds germinate.

Mix the seed with damp sand and put it in a plastic bag, then refrigerate for a month. It should then be sown while still damp.

(Iridaceae), lily (Liliaceae), daffodil (Amaryllidaceae), primula (Primulaceae), buttercup (Ranunculaceae), rose (Rosaceae), cow parsley (Umbelliferae) and gentian (Gentianaceae). These seeds should be sown in the autumn, to be chilled over the winter, or be treated by either of the stratification methods (see opposite, below).

If you are unsure about whether an individual species needs a cold spell before it will germinate, the most sensible policy is to sow some seed in the autumn and some in the spring, and keep records of the results. It is from such records that you will learn how to treat wild flower seed in the future. If you sow in the autumn and it germinates, protect the seedlings in a cold frame or greenhouse over the winter, to be pricked out in the spring. If it does not, it may need a cold spell to stimulate germination and will hopefully come up in the spring. There are a few wild flowers that will germinate only after two cold seasons, such as masterworts (*Astrantia*) and hellebores, although the latter will germinate quickly if sown absolutely fresh.

Some seed, notably members of the pea family (Leguminosae) such as vetches (*Vicia*), wild sweet peas (*Lathyrus*), lupins (*Lupinus*) and false indigos (*Baptisia*), is very tough and needs to be softened before sowing. Place the seed in a container and pour over it water that has just boiled, and then leave it to soak for 24 hours before sowing it.

Sowing seed in trays

For sowing seed in trays, I use an ordinary potting mix to which I add one third by volume of perlite, a light material that promotes aeration of the compost and good drainage; this also makes it easier to separate out the roots when pricking out. The seed compost must be sterilized and so must the seed trays themselves, otherwise they may be harbouring insects and fungal diseases.

Sow the seeds thinly on top of the compost. Seeds larger than a grain of sand should be covered with a light dusting of compost (without the addition of perlite), ideally no deeper than the size of the seed. Smaller seeds should be covered with a single layer of fine grit, which allows light to reach them. The pots or trays of sown seed should be watered by immer-

sion, and then allowed to drain for several hours. A brief sprinkling of water from a watering can fitted with a fine rose will help to settle the top of the compost, and will at the same time ensure good contact between seeds and compost.

Place the seed trays in a shaded situation outside; a cold frame is ideal. It is inadvisable to have them in a greenhouse, since high temperatures may inhibit germination, or cause delicate seedlings to dry out. If there is any risk of rodents or slugs eating the seedlings, enclose the trays or containers in plastic bags; this will also have the advantage of eliminating the need for watering and will keep out unwanted seed and moss spores.

Germination is always a magical moment, especially from seed that you have collected yourself. Once the seedlings are big enough, they can be pricked out and potted on; remember that not all of them will survive into adulthood, so pot on more than you need. It is usually too risky to plant out individual seedlings straight away, so it is safer to grow them on for a few months in small pots, about 8cm (3in) wide, and then plant them out in their final positions when you are confident that they are large enough to survive the occasional drought or nibbling slug.

Many seeds germinate only after a period of chilling, a process that prevents delicate seedlings from being exposed to freezing winter temperatures. The exquisite spring gentian (Gentiana verna) is one species, germinating profusely in spring after the cold of winter.

Cuttings

Two types of cutting are useful for wild flower gardeners: heel cuttings, taken in spring, and semi-ripe nodal cuttings, taken in summer and autumn.

Heel cuttings

Heel cuttings are pieces of new growth that are pulled off the crowns of herbaceous plants in spring. Plants that produce copious new side-shoots are the most suitable, for example goldenrods, bergamots, musk mallows and michaelmas daisies. Break off a firm young shoot, just expanding its first few leaves, by pulling downwards sharply; a modification is to cut off pieces with a knife. Plant in cuttings compost (ordinary sterilized compost mixed with half by volume of sand, grit or perlite, to improve drainage and aeration), spaced so that the leaves of individual cuttings do not quite touch each other – this reduces the spread of fungal infections. These spring cuttings usually root and grow very fast, making rooting powder usually unnecessary.

Nodal cuttings

Nodal cuttings are taken at a node, the point at which the leaf joins the stem, where there is generally a high concentration of the chemicals that promote growth. This technique is mostly used for woody plants, so it is suitable for many of the shrubby species that enjoy heathland habitats, like heathers and broom, as well as the low-growing woody plants that thrive in dry Mediterranean climates, like *Cistus*, rock roses and lavenders. And there are some exceptions among the herbaceous species, like the swamp hibiscus (*Hibiscus moscheutos*), cardinal flower (*Lobelia cardinalis*) and many spurges, whose stems are suitable for making nodal cuttings.

When taking semi-ripe cuttings, use a sharp knife and cut through the point just below the node. Each cutting needs to have at least one other node on it, as new growth will start from the dormant bud between the leaf and the stem. A single stem can be chopped into a number of cuttings, each with a node for growth of the roots and one for the new stems. Take off any leaves which might get buried in the compost and rot. Long lengths of stem above the upper node should be cut off as they are liable to decay. Dip the nodal cutting in rooting powder, then insert it in the cuttings compost (see above) sufficiently deep for it to hold itself upright securely.

Place pots or trays of cuttings in a light place, but out of direct sun – a shaded cold frame is ideal. Inspect them frequently by feeling the compost to see if watering is necessary. Remove dead leaves and failures to reduce the risk of fungal infections such as mould. Rooting may take several weeks but the young plants can then be gently acclimatized to full sun before being potted on or planted out.

Taking cuttings

Almost any species that forms clumps where there are multiple side-shoots is suitable for heel cuttings. The fresh new shoots on herbaceous plants in spring are very vigorous and can be used to create new plants in a surprisingly short time.

Nodal cuttings are a commonly used technique for propagating shrubby plants and those that form woody growth. Many species can be propagated quickly and easily by this means, such as rock rose and heathers, while others are much slower to root.

For a heel cutting, take a firm young shoot in thumb and forefinger and pull sharply down.

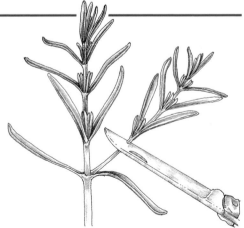

Take a nodal cutting using a sterilized sharp knife just below where a leaf joins the stem.

Division

Division is an excellent way of increasing many herbaceous wild flowers that spread sideways as well as grasses and some ferns. The easiest plants are those whose shoots spread along the soil surface, producing roots and shoots as they go, such as bugle or bergamot or the thelypteris ferns. New plants can be quickly identified and separated. Slightly more tricky are those plants that have a tighter crown, where it is less easy to establish that there are multiple growth points, for example yarrows, irises and goldenrods. In these cases, it is often easiest to dig the plant up or, in the event of an unmanageably large clump, to slice off a portion using a spade, and then to divide the clump into smaller pieces, making sure that each of them is a viable size.

The aim of division is to split a plant into as many viable new pieces as possible – that is, anything with a root and a shoot. Dividing plants can be a tough job: if cutting through with a trowel or spade does not work, try forcing the plant apart with two forks. In some cases, you can cut through with a sharp knife. Good-sized divisions, and certainly any piece with plenty of roots, can be treated as a new plant and put straight into its final place (see page 82). Small divisions, with only limited roots, are best cosseted a little, and planted out in a nursery bed or in pots of compost, until they are large enough to

Musk mallow (Malva moschata) *is a wild flower that can be propagated either from seed or cuttings but, as is usually the case, cutting-grown plants have a headstart and flower more quickly than seedlings. Like many herbaceous plants, musk-mallow cuttings are best taken in spring, from vigorous young growth.*

plant in the ground. The best time for division is spring, but vigorous growers like cranesbills and goldenrods can be divided at almost any time, provided the soil is sufficiently moist for them to establish themselves by spreading their roots.

Herbaceous plants that cannot be divided are those that have only a single crown, such as meadowsweets (*Filipendula vulgaris*) and many ferns. These plants can be reproduced only by seed or, in the case of ferns, by spores.

Dividing plants

Splitting herbaceous plants into smaller, viable sections is an immensely satisfying process. As a general rule, any plant that spreads by sending out new growth, including roots, from the side, is suitable. If the plant is divided at the start of the growing season, any piece that has both a root and a shoot can become a vigorous new plant within a month.

A large clump of cranesbill can be divided with a spade while still in the ground.

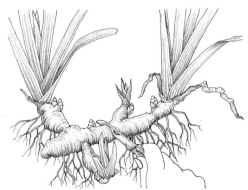

You may need to dig up plants like iris before slicing through the root or rhizome.

THROUGH THE SEASONS

Seasonal change is one of the most exciting aspects of gardening, and it puts us in touch with the rhythms of nature. How much more so in the wild flower garden, where wild plants are growing, flowering and seeding in front of our eyes. Different garden tasks need to be carried out each season, but you should never be too dogmatic about doing particular tasks at exact times of year; it is more important to understand your local climate and to work with the weather, rather than by your diary.

Observing the progress of the seasons is one of the most fascinating aspects of gardening: the endless cycle of growth, flowering, seeding and dying. Some flowers, like the daffodils and cowslips in this picture, are so strongly associated in our minds with the spring season that we almost rely on them to tell us the time of year. The daisies in the path, though, are a first hint of the summer to come.

Spring

Spring is the favourite time of year for many gardeners, especially if the winter has been a long and hard one. The first flowers of spring are among the most loved and appreciated of all and they remind us, even in those periods of cold and blustery weather when winter seems to have returned, that warmer days are just around the corner. Most spring wild flowers have bulbs or tuberous roots that store food reserves, enabling them to make rapid growth as soon as the soil begins to warm up. Woodland wild flowers are at their best in spring, flowering and growing before the leaves are on the trees.

Bulbs are many people's first choice – they combine colourful and reliable flowering with an extremely neat habit of growth – and there are many wild bulb species that naturalize quickly on a variety of soils. Crocuses and snowdrops (*Galanthus nivalis*) flower first, often before spring has properly started, followed by daffodils (*Narcissus*), scillas, tulips and many more. Of these, the wild crocus and daffodil species are the easiest to naturalize in most climates, although wild tulips are a possibility in dry, sunny places. Indeed, most wild bulb species are from regions with hot, dry summers, a fact which should be borne in mind when planning a garden in such a climate.

As well as bulbs there are those woodland wild flowers that sprout from tubers: anemones, trilliums, mertensias, bloodroots (*Sanguinaria*), and dutchman's breeches (*Dicentra* species). Many are slow growing and slow to propagate, which is why you should be sure that you buy nursery-propagated, not wild-collected stock. Some very hardy spring wild flowers do not have this tuberous habit, but seem to be able to grow whenever the winter weather is mild enough. Primroses (*Primula vulgaris*) and violets (*Viola* species) can even start flowering in mid-winter, and carry on well into the spring. These

Cyclamen coum *is one of the first flowers of the year, lasting through to spring.*

two are especially welcome for the relative speed with which they can spread and be propagated.

One of the wonders of a woodland in spring is the way that the ground is carpeted with a blend of colours, whether it is pale yellow primroses, violets and white anemones, or pink dutchman's breeches, white trilliums and blue mertensias. To get this blending right is the key to naturalistic wild flower planting.

Later in spring, almost as it turns into summer, the colour moves out of the deep woodland, into the lighter shade of hedgerows and glades. This is the time when open woodland is flooded with a sea of bluebells (*Hyacinthoides non-scripta*), or pink creeping phlox (*Phlox stolonifera*) and the hedgerows are full of red campions (*Silene dioica*) among the white stitchworts (*Stellaria graminea* and *S. holostea*) and the rampant mist-like white of cow parsley (*Anthriscus sylvestris*). In many places this can be the most colourful time of year, so you should consider carefully how you can make the most of it in the garden.

- Wild flower lawns can be left to grow and flower unchecked (see page 86) until the first days of summer, and should certainly be left to do so if they contain bulbs or early wild flowers. Otherwise they can be kept short (5cm/2in) until halfway through the spring, and then they can be left to grow.

- Spring wild flower meadows should be left uncut for the whole of spring.

- Summer meadows can be kept cut, to 7cm (2¾in), until late spring; this need be done only if you want to restrict the eventual height.

- The grass around bulbs should not be cut until the bulb leaves have yellowed, otherwise there may not be any flowers next year. If you are planning new projects, it might be wise to mark where the bulbs are, as you are unlikely to remember later in the year.

- Mulching should be carried out before the end of the spring (see page 89), to conserve moisture before the summer gets under way.

- The first weeding of the year needs to be done now (see page 72), to catch the weeds while they are still small.

- If you intend to clear any new land of weeds by means of black plastic (see page 72), this needs to be started now, after the windiest weather of winter is over but before the weeds have made much growth.

- Planting out can still be done (see page 82), at least in regions that do not experience dry summers, but the earlier in spring it takes place, the better the plants will establish.

- Wetlands and ponds (see page 92) can be planted or sown with wild flowers in late spring, after the danger of flooding or of excessively high water levels.

- Sow meadows and other large-scale wild flower features (see page 78) as soon as possible after the winter is over. Remember to provide some protection from birds.

- Cornfield and other annual sowings should be made in succession, that is, once a month in patches (see page 98), to get continuity of bloom over several weeks, rather than a single splash of colour.

● Small-scale sowings can be made now in trays or nursery beds (see page 101), for planting out later in spring or summer.

● Herbaceous plants can be divided (see page 101) just before they start back into growth. This is also the best time to divide clumps of the less vigorous species and grasses.

● Cuttings of many herbaceous plants can be taken by means of heel or semi-ripe nodal cuttings (see page 100), when their new shoots are still small, generally under 7cm (2¾in). If they are planted in loose, open compost and kept from drying out, cuttings can root and grow amazingly quickly.

Summer

Summer colour in the wild flower garden is basically provided by herbaceous perennials, in borders, wild flower lawns and meadows. Wild flower lawns, a refuge for daisies (*Bellis perennis*), clovers (*Trifolium* species) and other wild flowers often considered as weeds, are at their best in early summer, a rich assortment of colours spotting a green background. There will still be some colour to come, especially from the irrepressible self-heal (*Prunella vulgaris*).

Meadows tend to look their finest in the period around mid-summer, when the variety of wild flowers can be overwhelming. As time goes on, a meadow planting will be enriched by species joining it from outside the garden, these newcomers providing some of the greatest joys of meadow gardening. In the first few years the more vigorous species will be dominant, such as ox-eye daisy (*Leucanthemum vulgare*) and knapweeds (*Centaurea* species). These and many other members of the daisy family will attract butterflies and other insects to the meadow.

Ox-eye daisies and heartsease are two fast-growing summer wild flowers.

Butterflies are one of the main delights of the garden in summer and growing wild flowers is the best way to attract them.

As the summer progresses there will be fewer species flowering in a meadow, and the interest will shift towards the wild flowers of borders and hedgerow plantings. But you may still have real splashes of colour in the meadow from patches of cornfield and other annual wild flowers, sown in late spring.

Areas of wetland will be at their best in the period from mid-summer on. The sense of life that emanates from a pond or marsh on a warm summer's day, with the hum of insects and the luxuriant growth of the plants, is incredible. Wetland flowers start in early summer with the irises, which never seem to flower for long enough, moving on to yellow and purple loosestrifes (*Lysimachia* and *Lythrum*) and meadowsweets (*Filipendula*). In late summer the bold scarlet of cardinal flowers (*Lobelia cardinalis*) might be the focus of interest, along with mallows (*Malva* species).

By late summer it is the taller wild flowers that will provide most of the colour in the garden. Prairie plants such as lupins, false indigos (*Baptisia*) and the spectacular milkweed (*Asclepias tuberosa*), which will have looked good enough in mid-summer, are at their most majestic in late summer, with bluestems (*Andropogon*), ironweeds (*Vernonia*) and joe pye weeds (*Eupatorium*) well above head height. There are some smaller late-summer wild flowers too, perhaps the most colourful and useful being black-eyed susans (*Rudbeckia fulgida*) whose long season of dark-centred yellow flowers makes them one of the finest wild flowers for any garden, large or small.

With the trees in full leaf, there is little light for growth on the woodland floor, so many shade-lovers go dormant and few flower. There is plenty of scope for appreciating foliage in the shade of woodlands, however, in the contrasts of delicate ferns, marbled wild gingers (*Asarum*) and bold solomon's seals (*Polygonatum* and *Smilacina*). Areas of light shade, as in glades, clearings and hedgerows, are not without flowers in summer; indeed, the massed ranks of foxgloves (*Digitalis purpurea*) are one of the finest sights and one of the easiest to create in a wild flower garden. Tall woodland bellflowers (*Campanula*) and lilies are other possibilities for summer colour in areas of part-shade.

● Watering should not concern the wild flower gardener too much, as the aim is to grow plants that suit the conditions. Newly planted or sown areas might well need some irrigation, however. If you are watering seedlings, keep the spray gentle, otherwise they might be washed out of the ground all too easily.

● Summer is certainly a time to be vigilant about weeding (see page 72). Look out for invaders, especially in new plantings, and do not on any account let them seed.

● If you are considering clearing any areas for new projects, survey them carefully to see what is there, and how much is worth keeping. You may not do anything about it until the winter, but in winter you will not be able to recognize the plants that are there.

● Ground that is to be planted can be cleared of weeds and unwanted vegetation now (see page 70). Weedkillers work faster in warm weather and so do other methods such as rotovating and digging. Any weeds that you dig out will die rapidly in hot, dry weather.

● Seedlings and rooted cuttings from spring propagation (see pages 96–101) should be planted out now. They will need to be well watered on planting – filling the planting hole with water is a good way of doing this – and will possibly need irrigation, and certainly weeding, later in the season.

● New plantings made in summer should be mulched, after a good soaking, to conserve water and suppress weed seedlings (see page 89).

● Wild flower lawns need to be cut around mid-summer, otherwise they will turn into meadows. From then on, they should be cut every few weeks, to 8cm (3in).

● Spring meadows need to have their main cutting at mid-summer, to 5–8cm (2–3in), and to be kept down to around 8cm (3in) thereafter.

● Summer meadows should not be cut at all from now until autumn or winter. The only exception is where you want to restrict the height of tall, late-flowering wild flowers, in which case a mid-summer cut can be made.

● Remember to take away all clippings, in order to keep down soil fertility.

● From mid-summer onwards, you can start taking nodal cuttings of those wild flowers that can be propagated by this method (see page 100). They will need to be kept in a cool place and checked every few days for decaying leaves.

● Start thinking about seed collecting – earlier than you might expect. Some spring-flowering wild flowers will have formed ripe seed by mid-summer (see page 96 for methods of collecting).

The seedheads of old man's beard (Clematis vitalba) *drape shrubs in their autumn hues.*

Autumn

Brightly coloured leaves and berries on trees and shrubs are the chief glories of autumn, but there are quite a few meadow wild flowers that will flower until the first frosts, notably golden-rods (*Solidago* species) and michaelmas daisies (*Aster* species), and they can look spectacular against a background of red and orange trees in their autumn hues.

Many grasses also look their best in autumn, their full seedheads blowing in the wind, before the birds start eating them. It is a good idea to plan drifts of such grasses and wild flowers in a meadow, to prolong the season of flowering, specifically for this time of year.

Autumn should not be seen as the end of the gardening year, but in many ways a beginning. Traditionally it is the time of year for planting, as bare-rooted plants, especially trees and shrubs, establish much better if they can start growing roots over the winter in their new homes. Autumn and winter are, in many

senses, the natural and the most convenient time to lay out new areas of the garden.

● Clear ground for new planting (see page 70), as this is the ideal time to plant trees, shrubs and herbaceous plants. Most herbaceous wild flowers can be divided now too (see page 101), although less vigorous species and grasses should be left until spring.

● Sow meadows and other wild flower areas, unless you have done this in spring (see page 78). In regions without prolonged severe weather, the first half of autumn can be a good time to sow, and it is certainly the ideal time in areas which enjoy mild winters and hot, dry summers.

● If you have any wild flower seeds that you expect will need winter chilling before they germinate (see page 98), sow them now, either in nursery beds or in trays. Protect them from rodents by enclosing the trays in a clear plastic bag or putting them under cloches.

● Now is the time to tidy up the garden before the onset of winter. The dead stems of the summer's growth can be cut down and removed, to be composted and used elsewhere in the garden or shredded and used as a mulch. This mulch can be spread around new plantings as a weed-suppressant, or around woodland plants, which appreciate growing in organic matter (see page 89). It is better for wildlife, however, if the tidying up is left until later in the winter.

● Summer meadows cut at this time should be cut down to 8cm (3in).

● In areas which experience continual sub-zero winter temperatures, dead stems can be cut down to lie over and help insulate the gound-level buds of herbaceous plants.

● Dead leaves under trees can be swept up and gathered together to place around humus-loving woodland wild flowers. Shredding makes them easier to compact and thus less likely to blow around in the wind.

• Autumn and winter can be a good time for weeding, as there is less growth to get in your way. If weeds are a problem, consider mulching (see page 89) to stop their seeds from germinating in the future.

• Where spring bulbs are expected to come up, grass and other vegetation should be cut down and removed, so that the bulbs can have a headstart in the spring.

• Bulbs should be planted in autumn, the earlier the better, as they start to grow roots as soon as they are in the earth.

• Make small sowings of cornfield or annual meadow wild flowers (see page 84), leaving plenty of space for later spring sowings. These autumn-sown seeds will be the first flowers of next summer's cornfield.

Winter

There is no denying that winter is a relatively dull season in the garden, but this is no excuse for not trying to do something to brighten it up! There are plants that can bring beauty and interest to a garden in winter and in some ways the wild flower gardener is in the best position to take advantage of them.

Many grasses and herbaceous plants leave behind skeletal forms that have a gaunt beauty of their own in the architectural outlines of seedhead and stem, some stiff and upright, others bending before every breeze. Dead stems look best in meadow settings, where the variety of forms in what is left of the different plants contrast and complement each other, and their tendency to greater untidiness as winter moves on is less of a problem in a naturalistic environment. Seedheads have another purpose in the winter garden: they are a magnet for small, seed-eating birds like finches and thrushes.

The most attractive seedheads are those of the larger members of the daisy (Compositae) and scabious (Dipsaceae) families. Their size and

The spiky heads of teasels (Dipsacus fullonum) *stand out dramatically in frosty weather.*

heavier outline stand out among the smaller grass and wild flower stems. Two groups of thistle relatives – *Echinops* and *Eryngium* – have some of the best seedheads, and perhaps the finest is that of the teasel (*Dipsacus fullonum*). The joe pye weeds (*Eupatorium*) are also a feature in the winter, for the sheer size of their stems, topped with large, fluffy seedheads, have a distinct grandeur. Among the grasses, the largest are often the finest, partly because they have more presence in the landscape and partly because their physical bulk means that they stay upright for longer. The *Miscanthus* grasses, which originate from Japan, are worth mixing with wild flowers for their winter appearance alone; their impressive height (up to 2.5m/8ft in some varieties) providing a focus of interest among the lower-growing plants. The seedheads almost glow with silver when backlit by low, winter sun. Stems and seedheads are especially appreciated in the snow, as little will settle on them, and they can be the only parts of the garden visible against a white blanket.

Berries are the main feature of shrubs in winter, often accompanied by flocks of hungry birds – but you will not have both for very long. Diversity of planting is the key to keeping the display of berries and birds going for as long as possible, as birds are highly selective and tend to eat the berries of some plants before moving on to those of others.

As far as winter flowers are concerned, much depends on the severity of the local climate. In areas without constant snow cover there are possibilities: elegant and sinister hellebores (*Helleborus foetidus*), the extraordinary little pink *Cyclamen coum* and snowdrops (*Galanthus nivalis*), all of which can be easily naturalized in shaded places in the garden.

• Carry on the autumn's work of planning and planting. Winter is a good time to carry out major projects as there is less vegetation to get in the way of operations such as earth moving, digging and planting. Transplanted shrubs and perennials are not going to dry out, so this is still a good time to plant.

• Towards the end of the winter the garden will be looking its scruffiest; even the most majestic teasel stems will be gale-blown and rain-bedraggled. If you have not already done so, choose a fine day on which to tidy up, cutting meadows and removing all the dead stems (see page 84).

• Many herbaceous wild flowers can be divided and replanted now: they will be more manageable than when accompanied by a metre or more of stem, and they will establish better. Leave the division of less vigorous plants and grasses until spring, however.

• The most pleasurable aspect of gardening in the winter is dreaming about the possibilities offered by the coming season – preferably sitting by a warming fire. This is the time to read garden books and plough through seed catalogues, to fantasize about what could be and to make plans for what will be.

KEY PLANTS

Selecting the wild flowers to include here from such a vast number of species and geographical regions has not been easy. What follows is a guide to the plants that I find are the most rewarding. All are perennials; annuals certainly have their place, but I feel that permanence and reliability are the cornerstone of wild flower gardening. The flowers listed are easy and quick to establish, giving rapid results, with an emphasis on a long and colourful season of flower and, wherever possible, elegant and attractive foliage.

Of all wild flowers, foxgloves (Digitalis purpurea) combine the virtues of ease of growth and spectacular colour most effectively. To do well, they need light shade and a soil that is not too alkaline, when they will self-seed to produce colonies like this.

Campanula
rotundifolia (harebell)

Achillea millefolium
(Yarrow)

Yarrow is a tough and vigorous perennial plant which often does well where others do not thrive, although the disadvantage is that it does have a tendency to swamp less vigorous plants. It has flat-topped white flowers in mid-summer, but the dark ferny foliage looks good all year round. There are also cultivars available in reds, yellows and pinks, and other species, which are all as easy and rewarding to grow. An excellent meadow plant. **Size** H and S: 30–60cm/1–2ft. **Aspect** Anywhere reasonably sunny. **Hardiness** Fully hardy. **Soil** Any. **Propagation** Division; seed. **Distribution** Europe; introduced to North America, possibly unwisely as it can spread vigorously to the detriment of the native wild flowers. **Planting partners** Strong growers like cranesbills (*Geranium*), knapweeds (*Centaurea*), goldenrods (*Solidago*).

Ajuga reptans
(Bugle)

A very versatile little wild flower, suitable for hedgerows, damp meadows or half-shade, that looks good over a long period. It has clear blue flowers in late spring but the bronze-coloured leaves are a feature throughout the summer. Runners ensure that it spreads quickly and freely.
Size H: 10–15cm/4–6in; S: 60cm/2ft.
Aspect Sun or shade. **Hardiness** Fully hardy. **Soil** Damp and rich. **Propagation** Division; seed. **Distribution** Europe. **Planting partners** Small ferns such as lady fern (*Athyrium filix-femina*), cranesbills (*Geranium*), violets (*Viola*), primrose (*Primula vulgaris*), lesser celandine (*Ranunculus ficaria*).

Althaea see under *Hibiscus*

Anemone

Wood anemones are classic spring flowers, forming a delicate white carpet for great expanses of forest floor. There are three very similar species bearing this name: *A. nemorosa* in Europe, and *A. caroliniana* and *A. quinquefolia* in North America. *A. blanda* has a variety of different colour forms, including blue, pink, white.
Size H: 15cm/6in; S: 20cm/8in.
Aspect Shade. **Hardiness** Fully hardy. **Soil** Fertile, rich in organic matter. **Propagation** Seed, which is slow to germinate; division of tubers. **Planting partners** Small spring flowers like violets (*Viola*), primrose (*Primula vulgaris*) and small bulbs such as *Scilla* and *Chionodoxa*.

Asclepias
(Milkweed)

Beloved of butterflies, milkweeds add a touch of the unusual to the wild flower garden with their clusters of strange 'horned' flowers. They are at their most colourful in mid-summer, but often go on longer. Butterfly milkweed (*A. tuberosa*) is the finest, with brilliant orange flowers on 60cm (2ft) stems. The swamp milkweed (*A. incarnata*) has white or pink flowers on 90cm (3ft) stems. Common milkweed (*A. syriaca*) is similar, and has attractive broad leaves, but can run amok. All are good meadow plants.
Size S: 30cm/1ft. **Aspect** Full sun. **Hardiness** Fully hardy. **Soil** Any well-drained soil. **Propagation** Fresh seed; cuttings; transplant carefully as the long taproots are easily damaged. **Distribution** North America. **Planting partners** Summer meadow or prairie flowers like lupins and false indigo (*Baptisia*).

Aster
(Michaelmas daisy)

Also known as new england aster, (*A. novae-angliae*) is a much-loved harbinger of autumn, with mauve to blue daisies on lanky 90cm–1.5m (3–5ft) stems. A vigorous grower, it is best in a meadow, prairie or a large wild border. Other asters flowering in late summer until the first frosts include: white wood aster (*A. divaricatus*), excellent for shady areas and growing 30–60cm (1–2ft) high; frost flower aster (*A. ptarmicoides*), growing to 30–45cm (1–1½ft) with smaller, white flowers and useful for dry places;

and heath aster (*A. ericoides*), also a dry land plant, a magnificent mass of white, up to 90cm (3ft) high and as much across.

Size S: 60–90cm/2–3ft. **Aspect** Best in full sun, but will tolerate a little shade. **Hardiness** Fully hardy. **Soil** Any, but less fertile soil will mean more compact growth. **Distribution** North America; introduced to Europe. **Planting partners** Strong, late wild flowers like goldenrods (*Solidago*), *Rudbeckia*, joe pye weeds (*Eupatorium*), ironweeds (*Vernonia*); dramatic grasses.

Baptisia
(False indigo)

These distinctive and strong-growing plants help other plants by introducing nitrogen to the soil. Blue false indigo (*Baptisia australis*) has blue pea flowers in late spring and stylish, blue-green foliage in summer. Prairie false indigo (*B. leucantha*) has white flowers against lovely dark foliage. These are big, long-lived plants, sometimes slow to establish, so they should be placed carefully, as moving them later will do them (and you) considerable injury. Their size restricts their use to the back of the border and large meadow or prairie schemes.

Size H and S: 90cm/3ft. **Aspect** Full sun. **Hardiness** Will not survive very severe winters. **Soil** Any well-drained. **Propagation** Seed, softened in very hot water. **Distribution** Central and southern USA; introduced to gardens in Europe. **Planting partners** Large prairie grasses and wild flowers such as sunflowers (*Helianthus, Heliopsis*), goldenrods (*Solidago*), *Coreopsis, Asclepias*.

Bee balm see *Monarda*

Bellflower see *Campanula*

Bellis perennis
(Daisy)

One of the most common of all wild flowers, the daisy is easy to establish. Nevertheless, the beauty of a lawn scattered with their white and yellow flowers from late spring into summer is undeniable.

Size H: 10cm/4in; S: 8cm/3in. **Aspect** Full sun. **Soil** Any well-drained. **Distribution** Europe; introduced to North America. **Planting partners** Does not tolerate competition, so plant only with other small growers like cowslip (*Primula veris*), birdsfoot trefoil (*Lotus corniculatus*).

Bergamot see *Monarda*

Black-eyed susan see *Rudbeckia*

Bluebell see *Hyacinthoides*

Bugle see *Ajuga reptans*

Buttercup see *Ranunculus*

Campanula
(Bellflower)

Bellflowers are a useful source of mid-summer blue or mauve. The harebell (*C. rotundifolia*) is one of the most charming, with graceful pale blue bells on thread-like stems. It establishes well on poor, dry soils in sun, provided there is not too much compe-

Anemone nemorosa
(wood anemone)

tition from larger plants. It grows to 13cm (5in) high and spreads as much across. The clustered bellflower (*C. glomerata*) has dark purple flowers in a tight cluster, and needs similar conditions. It grows 20–30cm (8–12in) high and spreads to 30cm (1ft). Several bellflowers prefer woodland conditions. The giant bellflower (*C. latifolia*) is one of the best, with mauve-blue, sometimes white, flowers on 60cm (2ft) stems. The nettle-leaved bellflower (*C. trachelium*) is similar but coarser-looking with paler flowers.

Aspect Depends on the species. **Hardiness** Fully hardy. **Soil** Prefer lime. **Propagation** Division; seed. **Distribution** Europe; North America. **Planting partners** Other wild flowers of similar size and vigour, such as foxglove (*Digitalis purpurea*) and masterwort (*Astrantia major*).

Campion see *Silene*

Centaurea nigra
(common knapweed)

Centaurea
(Knapweed)

Knapweeds are similar to thistles but without the prickles, flowering in mid-summer, but often carrying on longer, and much appreciated by butterflies and bees. They are all vigorous meadow wild flowers. Common knapweed (*C. nigra*) has dark pink-mauve flowerheads. Greater knapweed (*C. scabiosa*) is a wonderfully showy plant with big pink flowerheads and attractive divided leaves; a meadow full of these is a magnificent sight. Mountain knapweed (*C. montana*) has large blue flowerheads, above grey felty leaves. There are many other species that make excellent wild garden plants. **Size** H: 30–60cm/1–2ft; S: 20–60cm/8in–2ft, depending on species. **Aspect** Full sun. **Hardiness** Fully hardy. **Soil** Well-drained, preferably limy. **Propagation** Seed. **Distribution** Europe. **Planting partners** Other strong-growing meadow wild flowers, such as members of the daisy family, and 30–60cm (1–2ft) tall grasses, scabious, cranesbills (*Geranium*).

Chrysogonum virginianum
(Green and gold)

One of the few members of the daisy family that tolerates light shade, green and gold is first-class compact ground cover. There are various cultivars available, some more compact than others. Yellow flowers are produced over a long season in spring and often into the summer months as well.
Size H: 15–45cm/6in–1½ft, depending on the variety; S: 30cm/1ft. **Aspect** Sun or half-shade. **Hardiness** Fully hardy. **Soil** Well-drained, preferably poor. **Propagation** Division is best. **Distribution** Eastern USA. **Planting partners** Other late-spring flowering and low-growing woodland wild flowers like dwarf crested iris (*Iris cristata*), meadow cranesbill (*Geranium pratensis*), *Heuchera*, *Tiarella*.

Clover see *Trifolium*

Coneflower see *Rudbeckia*

Coreopsis
(Tickseed)

Like miniature reflections of the sun itself, the yellow daisies of *Coreopsis*, produced early to mid-summer, are one of the most useful groups of easy wild flowers. The compact, thread-leaved coreopsis (*C. verticillata*), which grows to 45–75cm (1½–2½ft) high, has light yellow flowers and is the best for border and tidier areas. Dwarf tickseed (*C. auriculata*), which grows to no more than 30–45cm (1–1½ft), is one of the few daisies that will do well in shade. For meadows and prairies the larger, less compact species are more suitable, such as lance-leaved coreopsis (*C. lanceolata*) and stiff coreopsis (*C. palmata*). They will easily reach a metre high and seed readily.
Size S: Around 30cm/1ft, regardless of height. **Aspect** Full sun. **Hardiness** Fully hardy. **Soil** Any well-drained. **Propagation** Seed. **Distribution** North America. **Planting partners** Grasses, at least 30cm (1ft) tall, and other meadow plants, especially purple flowered species such as cranesbills (*Geranium*) and bergamots (*Monarda*).

Cowslip see *Primula*

Cranesbill see *Geranium*

Daisy see *Bellis perennis*

Daucus carota
(Wild carrot)

Vigorously growing and avidly self-seeding, this meadow plant is a blessing on difficult sites where there is competition from weeds. The flat-topped lacy white flowers are undeniably attractive. The ferny foliage and seedheads look good too after the midsummer flowering.

Size H: 45–60cm/1½–2ft; S: 30cm/1ft. **Aspect** Sun, but tolerates some shade. **Hardiness** Fully hardy. **Soil** Any, especially dry and poor. **Distribution** Europe; introduced to North America. **Planting partners** Anything that is fairly tough so it is not overwhelmed: the lovely blue of wild chicory (*Cichorium intybus*) is a perfect match, aesthetically and ecologically, as well as meadow cranesbill (*Geranium pratense*) and other large cranesbills.

———————

Dead-nettle see *Lamium*

Devil's bit scabious
see *Succisa pratensis*

———————

Digitalis purpurea
(Foxglove)

One of the most spectacular wild flower sights is an area of light woodland full of these tall spires of deep pink. Foxgloves are at their best in areas where the soil has been disturbed by forestry activities. They are biennials, living for two years and dying after flowering in mid-summer, but setting masses of seed. To keep foxgloves going, the soil needs forking over occasionally to discourage perennial grasses and wild flowers, and to give the scattered seed a chance to germinate. This species is the brightest, but there are others, all easy although short-lived, for light woodland.

Size H: 60cm–1.5m/2–5ft; S: 45cm/1½ft. **Aspect** Sun or half-shade. **Hardiness** Fully hardy. **Soil** Well-drained, acid or neutral. **Propagation** Seed. **Distribution** West and central Europe. **Planting partners** Ferns (see page 114), columbines (*Aquilegia*), cranesbills (*Geranium*), bluebells (*Hyacinthoides*), spurges (*Euphorbia*), woodland bellflowers (*Campanula*).

———————

Dog's tooth violet see *Erythronium*

Dropwort see *Filipendula*

Eastern wild lupin
see *Lupinus perennis*

———————

Echinacea purpurea
(Purple coneflower)

A very showy, mid-summer-blooming member of the daisy family, whose large flowers have distinct reflexed pink petals. Its sturdy good looks make it invaluable for borders as well as meadows and prairies.

Size H: 120cm/4ft; S: 45cm/1½ft. **Aspect** Sun. **Hardiness** Fully hardy. **Soil** Any well-drained. **Distribution** North America; introduced to gardens in Europe. **Planting partners** Milkweeds (*Asclepias*), large grasses, blazing star (*Liatris*), *Coreopsis*, yellow coneflower (*Ratibida*).

———————

Erythronium
(Trout lily, dog's tooth violet)

These spring-flowering woodland bulbs have attractive mottled leaves and flowers with slightly reflexed

Daucus carota
(wild carrot)

petals. *E. dens-canis* is a small species with flowers that are either cream or lavender; *E. umbilicatum* has yellow and purple flowers; *E. albidum* is pure white. They will spread over time.

Size H: 10–25cm/4–10in; S: 15cm/6in. **Aspect** Shade. **Hardiness** Fully hardy. **Soil** Moist, acidic, rich in organic matter. **Propagation** Division of clumps; seed, which is slow to germinate. **Distribution** North America. **Planting partners** *Trillium*, bloodroots (*Sanguinaria*), *Dicentra*, creeping phlox (*Phlox stolonifera*).

Filipendula ulmaria
(meadowsweet)

Eupatorium

(Joe pye weed, hemp agrimony,
snakeroot, mist flower)

The glory of these wild flowers is the soft, mist-like nature of their flower-heads seen *en masse*, especially when covered in butterflies in late summer. Joe pye weed, a classic prairie flower, is a name that refers to several very similar species, which all have fuzzy, pale pink flowers atop tall and magnificent stems. *E. maculatum* and *E. fistulosum* are the biggest (to 2.5m/8ft); *E. purpureum* and *E. dubium* are slightly smaller (90cm–2m/3–6½ft). The large joe pyes are unbeatable for adding scale and majesty to a border. Hemp agrimony (*E. cannabinum*) is similar, growing to 120cm (4ft), but much more shade-tolerant. There are two smaller species (to 75cm/2½ft) suitable for light shade: mist flower (*E. coelestinum*) has delicate blue flowers, and white snakeroot (*E. rugosum*) has white flowers. Both look superb when grown on a large scale in light wood-land. They seed and spread easily.

Size S: Generally half the height (see above). **Aspect** Sun, unless mentioned. **Hardiness** Hardy apart from *E. coelestinum* which will not survive less than -5°C/25°F. **Soil** Any, preferably moist. **Propagation** Division; seed. **Distribution** North America; *E. cannabinum* is European. **Planting partners** Late-flowering vigorous wild flowers like goldenrods (*Solidago*), ironweeds (*Vernonia*), *Rudbeckia*.

Euphorbia

(Spurge)

Spurges are curious flowers, their main feature being the green bracts around the flower itself. They are widely grown for the subtle yellow-green shades they bring to borders of more conventionally coloured plants. Given the ease and vigour of their growth, many are suitable as wild garden plants. Wood spurge (*E. amygdaloides*) is valued for its ability to look good at all times of year in difficult, dry, shady conditions. It has interesting dark leaves and fresh green flowerheads in early spring. *E. robbiae* is similar, with a neater habit, dark glossy leaves and a fearsome ability to spread well in dry situations. The marsh spurge (*E. palustris*), which prefers moist ground, forms a compact plant with pale green spring flowers and brilliant orange autumn foliage.

Size H: 30–75cm/1–2½ft; S: 45–75cm/1½–2½ft. **Aspect** Sun or shade. **Hardiness** Fully hardy. **Soil** Any. **Propagation** Division; seed; cuttings. **Distribution** Europe.

Planting partners Spurges look good with most wild flowers but pale yellow and purple companions in spring, such as primrose (*Primula vulgaris*) and violets (*Viola*), are especially lovely.

Evening primrose see *Oenothera*

Fair maid of france see *Ranunculus*

False dragonhead
see *Physostegia virginiana*

False indigo see *Baptisia*

Ferns

Predominantly creatures of the shade, ferns are unrivalled as foliage plants for dark places. Lady fern (*Athyrium filix-femina*) is a medium-sized (45cm/1½ft) fern, suitable for most shady spots. *Thelypteris* species are of a similar size but spread particularly well, in time making a ground cover of fresh green lace. Polypody (*Polypodium vulgare*) is a small (30cm/1ft) species with relatively undivided fronds, that will not only grow on the ground but also scamper up tree trunks in moist climates. For cool, damp soils, the ostrich fern (*Matteucia struthiopteris*) is superb, forming a rosette up to 120cm (4ft) tall. Very similar, but coping well in dry shade is the male fern (*Dryopteris filix-mas*). Another ever-green fern tolerant of dry shade is the christmas fern (*Polystichum acrostichoides*), which grows to 45cm (1½ft). **Aspect** Half to full shade (but not dark) for most ferns; the drier the soil, the more shade they will need. **Hardi-**

ness Depends on the species. **Soil** Most need a soil that does not dry out readily. **Propagation** Some can be divided, otherwise propagate by spores, a somewhat specialized business. **Distribution** Depends on the species. **Planting partners** Other woodland plants; white flowers look lovely and cool; plants with contrasting foliage, such as *Pachysandra*, *Asarum*, *Arisaema*, *Ajuga*, *Arum*.

Filipendula
(Meadowsweet, dropwort, queen of the prairie)

The softness and subtlety of the flowers and their sweet fragrance make these mid-summer wild flowers very special. Meadowsweet (*F. ulmaria*) will grow profusely in damp ground, with cream flowers atop a stem reaching from 60–120cm (2–4ft). Dropwort (*F. vulgaris*), with fluffy white flowers and ferny foliage, will grow on drier ground, but only to 45cm (1½ft). Queen of the prairie (*F. rubra*) is pink and tops 2m (6½ft).

Size S: 20–30cm/8–12in. **Aspect** Sun or light shade. **Hardiness** Fully hardy. **Soil** Any, preferably moist. **Propagation** Division; seed. **Distribution** North America; Europe. **Planting partners** Best on their own.

Fire pink see *Silene*

Flag see *Iris*

Flower of jove see *Lychnis*

Foxglove see *Digitalis purpurea*

Geranium
(Cranesbill)

Tough, adaptable and colourful, cranesbills will spread well but without over-extending their welcome. Without doubt one of the finest groups of plant for the wild flower garden, they are equally good as denizens of the respectable border. There they usually form solid clumps of foliage, which do a good job of smothering weeds, but in meadow settings they will trail.

Geranium endressii is a good, medium-sized (30–45cm/1–1½ft) pink species that spreads well; *G. versicolor* is very similar, with pretty veined flowers; the deep pink *G.* 'Claridge Druce' is a larger cultivar (75cm/2½ft) that will do battle with the strongest weeds and self-seed well. These three flower from late spring to late summer. Another good spreader is *G. macrorrhizum*, with pink flowers in late spring, growing to 45cm (1½ft). One of the most compact, 30cm (1ft) tall, is the early summer-flowering bloody cranesbill (*G. sanguineum*), usually a rather loud pink, but with pale pink and mauve forms. *G. ibericum* and *G. × magnificum* are bushy growers, to 60cm (2ft), with purple flowers in mid-summer; *G.* 'Johnson's Blue' is a similar size with deep blue flowers. The meadow cranesbill (*G. pratensis*) has pale blue flowers in early summer; it is a fine meadow plant of 30–75cm (1–2½ft), but tends to collapse without the support of other plants. The pink-flowered mountain cranesbill (*G. pyrenaicum*) needs to grow with other plants as well, to support its trailing stems. The mourning widow (*G. phaeum*) is a bushy (to

60cm/2ft) species, with mysterious dark flowers in late spring. Flowering at the same time is the wood cranesbill (*G. sylvaticum*), at 45–60cm (1½–2ft) tall, with mauve, pink or white flowers.

Size S: Usually half as much again as the height, but plants will gradually build up into large clumps. **Aspect** Sun or half-shade. **Hardiness** Fully hardy. **Soil** Any soil, but they do best in moist and fertile ground. **Propagation** Division; seed, but which is time-consuming to collect. **Distribution** Europe; introduced to gardens in North America. **Planting partners** Ferns (see page 114), taller herbaceous wild flowers, meadowsweet (*Filipendula*), hemp agrimony (*Eupatorium cannabinum*), bellflowers (*Campanula*).

Giant chickweed see *Stellaria*

Goldenrod see *Solidago*

Athyrium filix-femina (lady fern)

Hyacinthoides non-scripta (bluebells)

Grasses

Grasses form the majority of the plants in meadows and prairies, but they need not be seen as merely a background for the wild flowers. Propagated by seed or division, grasses (and their close relatives the sedges and rushes) are plants of great beauty in their own right, often with attractive foliage and elegant flower and seedheads. These seedheads come into their own in the winter, especially if everything else in the garden is covered by a thick blanket of snow.

The grasses mentioned in the prairie section (see pages 50–1) are all eminently suitable as feature plants in other kinds of wild flower garden or border, as is beach panic grass (see pages 66–7). Some large and dramatic upright grasses that will add impact and height to any planting in the sun are: *Miscanthus sinensis*, *M. floridulus* and *Spodiopogon sibiricus*, growing to between 1.5–2m (5–6½ft), and higher in warm climates. The pennisetum grasses are among the most beautiful of those that grow lower, to no more than 90cm (3ft), but arch out with sprays of graceful and softly textured seedheads. Purple moor grass (*Molinia caerulea*) is popular for poor, acidic soils, its dense tufts growing to 45cm (1½ft). There are few grasses suitable for shade, but *Deschampsia caespitosa* and *Chasmanthium latifolium* are two, and they are strikingly different. *Deschampsia* grows up to 75cm (2½ft), and is wonderfully delicate, with its huge sprays of tiny flowers; it needs acid soil and spreads rapidly. *Chasmanthium* grows to over 90cm (3ft) and has broad leaves and large clusters of oat-like seed.

Wood rushes (*Luzula*) are very similar to grasses but tend to favour moister environments. Quietly attractive plants, they often thrive in places too shady for most grasses. Snowy woodrush (*L. nivea*) has pretty white flowerheads on 60cm (2ft) stems in late spring and slightly hairy, dark green grassy foliage. Greater woodrush (*L. sylvatica*) has less attractive brown flowers but rather fine dark green leaves in dense tufts. It grows to 75cm (2½ft) in flower and spreads persistently, but not aggressively.

Weeping sedge (*Carex pendula*) is a bold and majestic plant, 90cm (3ft) high, tailor-made for waterside planting in sun or light shade. It has ribbed leaves and pendent brown flower/seed heads which are a feature from spring right through until autumn.

Green and gold
see *Chrysogonum virginianum*

Heliopsis helianthoides
(Ox-eye)

One of the best of the innumerable yellow 'sunflowers' that celebrate midsummer, ox-eye can carry on until early autumn. There are several cultivars available, which might be better plants used in a border than the original species, which makes a fine meadow or prairie plant.

Size H: 1.2–1.5m/4–5ft; S: 75cm/2½ft. **Aspect** Sun. **Hardiness** Hardy. **Soil** Any that does not get too dry. **Propagation** Seed. **Distribution** North America. **Planting partners** Other large daisy flowers, especially of contrasting colour like purple coneflower (*Echinacea purpurea*), blazing stars (*Liatris*) and bergamots (*Monarda*).

Helleborus foetidus
(Hellebore)

All the hellebores make good wild garden plants, given their robust habit, attractive evergreen leaves and winter flowers, but this is the best. It forms a stately mound of dark glossy leaves, with its curious green flowers at the top, from mid-winter on. It can self-seed rapidly.

Size H and S: 90cm/3ft. **Aspect** Sun or shade. **Hardiness** Fully hardy. **Soil** Any well-drained. **Propagation** Division; seed, which is prolific but must be sown fresh. **Distribution** Europe. **Planting partners** Spurges (*Euphorbia*), ferns (see page 114), cranesbills (*Geranium*), foxgloves (*Digitalis*).

Hemp agrimony see
Eupatorium

Hibiscus

The huge blooms of these showy wild flowers bring a touch of the exotic to the wild flower garden. *Hibiscus moscheutos* has large, open flowers in every shade from red to white on 1.5m (5ft) stems. There are several other herbaceous species of hibiscus; the most spectacular is *Hibiscus coccineus*, whose scarlet flowers wave from the top of 2.5m (8ft) stems. It does not like cold winters, though. Closely related is the marsh mallow (*Althaea officinalis*), which produces delicate pink flowers on strong 90cm (3ft) stems. All the above species make good border, meadow or wetland plants, flowering in late summer.

Size S: 60cm/2ft. **Aspect** Full sun. **Hardiness** Will not survive below -8°C/18°F. **Soil** Moist. **Propagation** Cuttings; seed. **Distribution** *Hibiscus*: eastern North America; *Althaea*: Europe. **Planting partners** Need to be large and dramatic so that they are not overwhelmed visually; try large grasses, ironweeds (*Vernonia*), joe pye weeds (*Eupatorium*).

Hyacinthoides
(Bluebell)

Bluebells (*H. non-scripta*, syn. *Endymion non-scriptus*) can be a spectacular woodland sight in late spring. Fortunately they spread much more quickly than most bulbs in the garden. The spanish bluebell (*H. hispanica*) is a bulkier plant that forms dense clumps.

Size H: 20–30cm/8–12in; S: 10cm/4in. **Aspect** Shade. **Hardiness** Fully hardy. **Soil** Light, preferably acid. **Propagation** Buy bulbs; seed is prolific but will take several months to germinate and several years to flower. **Distribution** Europe. **Planting partners** Red campion (*Silene dioica*), stichworts (*Stellaria*), cow parsley (*Anthriscus sylvestris*) and related wild flowers, primroses (*Primula vulgaris*).

Iris
(Flag)

Irises are truly beautiful flowers and, as a group, extraordinarily versatile. The wild flower gardener is mainly interested in those that grow well in water and wet soils. Yellow flag (*I. pseudacorus*) is a large (90cm–1.5m/3–5ft), strong-growing plant of pond margins. Other water irises include blue flag (*I. versicolor*), blue-violet in colour and 60–90cm (2–3ft) tall, southern blue flag (*I. virginica*), similar in size with paler flowers, and the slender blue flag (*I. prismatica*) which grows to a height of only 30–60cm (1–2ft) and has much more graceful blue-violet flowers.

There are few shade-tolerant irises, but the crested iris (*I. cristata*) is a delightful dwarf (10–20cm/4–8in), with blue flowers that can be used as ground cover on shaded acid soils. All are late-spring flowering.

Size S: 45cm/1½ft. **Aspect** Sun. **Hardiness** Hardy; southern blue flag possibly less so. **Soil** Best in wet ground or pond margins. **Propagation** Division; seed is possible but will take years to flower. **Distribution** North America, except for yellow flag which is originally European. **Planting partners** Other wetland plants that offer a contrast in foliage such as loosestrifes (*Lysimachia* and *Lythrum*), marsh marigolds (*Caltha*), and waterside ferns like *Osmunda*.

Ironweed see *Vernonia*

Jacob's ladder
see *Polemonium caeruleum*

Joe pye weed see *Eupatorium*

Knapweed see *Centaurea*

Knautia see under *Scabiosa*

Iris cristata
(crested iris)

Lamium
(Dead-nettle)

Dead-nettles are virtually foolproof wild flowers for a long season of spring and early summer colour. In addition there are many cultivars with attractive, variegated, evergreen foliage. They are ideal for filling in awkward corners in partly shaded spots. The white dead-nettle (*L. album*) is perhaps the best, but there is also the spotted dead-nettle (*L. maculatum*), with pink flowers, and the short-lived, but always regenerating, red dead-nettle (*L. purpureum*). Yellow archangel (*L. galeobdolon* syn. *Lamiastrum galeobdolon*) is of similar habit.
Size H: 20–50cm/8–20in; S: 60cm/2ft. **Aspect** Sun or half-shade. **Hardiness** Fully hardy. **Soil** Any. **Propagation** Division; cuttings. **Distribution** Europe; introduced elsewhere. **Planting partners** Grows best with other vigorous spreaders like bugles (*Ajuga*), cranesbills (*Geranium*), red campion (*Silene dioica*).

Lathyrus see under ***Vicia***

Lesser celandine see ***Ranunculus***

Leucanthemum vulgare
(Ox-eye daisy)

This white and yellow daisy is a classic mid-summer wild flower. It is very vigorous and can run riot over new meadows in their first year or so. Ideal for rough ground, it should be kept away from more delicate plants.
Size H: 45–75cm/1½–2½ft; S: 60–90cm/2–3ft. **Aspect** Sun. **Hardiness** Fully hardy. **Soil** Any, though poorer soils will restrain its growth. **Propagation** Division; seed. **Distribution** Europe; introduced to North America. **Planting partners** Need to be strong growers such as yarrows (*Achillea*), goldenrods (*Solidago*), meadow cranesbill (*Geranium pratense*).

Lilium
(Lily)

Lilies are majestic plants, slow to establish, but well worth the effort. The best for shaded wild gardens are the martagon lily (*L. martagon*), with reflexed pink flowers, and the turk's cap (*L. superbum*), which has similarly shaped orange flowers dotted with purple. Canada lily (*L. canadense*) is a beautiful yellow for sunnier gardens. The above flower in mid-summer.
Size H: 90cm–2m/3–6½ft; S: 30–45cm/1–1½ft. **Hardiness** Hardy. **Soil** Moist, but well-drained, rich in organic matter. **Propagation** Seed, which is slow to germinate. **Distribution** North America; Europe. **Planting partners** Best with lower-growing, compact plants, such as cranesbills (*Geranium*), so as not to distract from their elegant beauty.

Lupinus perennis
(Eastern wild lupin)

A field of lupins in early summer is a sea of shimmering blue. An excellent meadow or prairie plant, its growth is compact enough to make it a good border plant too.
Size H: 30–60cm/1–2ft; S: 60cm/2ft. **Aspect** Full sun. **Hardiness** Fully hardy. **Soil** Any well-drained. **Propagation** Seed, which needs soaking in very hot water first. Transplant only young plants. **Distribution** Eastern North America. **Planting partners** Other summer-flowering prairie plants, such as milkweeds (*Asclepias*). Yellow 'sunflower' plants such as *Heliopsis* associate well with the blue.

Lychnis
(Rose campion, flower of jove, ragged robin)

Fast-growing and rapidly seeding, these cheerful, pink wild flowers are easy to establish in meadows or borders. Rose campion (*L. coronaria*)

Lychnis flos-cuculi
(ragged robin)

has silver-haired foliage and bright pink flowers; flower of jove (*L. flos-jovis*) is similar but with flowers in an extra-ordinary shade of deep cerise-purple; ragged robin (*L. flos-cuculi*) has pink flowers with unusual, deeply fringed petals. All flower in early summer. **Size** H: 45–90cm/1½–3ft; S: 45cm/1½ft. **Aspect** Sun. **Hardiness** Fully hardy. **Soil** Any; ragged robin prefers it damp. **Propagation** Division; seed. **Distribution** Europe; introduced else-where. **Planting partners** Ragged robin consorts well with other wild flowers of damp places, such as lady's smock (*Cardamine pratensis*) and fritil-lary (*Fritillaria meleagris*). The others look superb with just grasses. All are complemented by white flowers.

Mallow see *Malva*

Malva
(Mallow)

Easy and rewarding, mallows will hap-pily spread their pink flowers with gay abandon over any sunny place. Musk mallow (*M. moschata*) is the most attractive, with delicate pink flowers on a plant that grows 30–60cm (1–2ft) tall, an ideal meadow plant; *M. alcea* is almost identical but twice the size. The common mallow (*M. sylvestris*) is an opportunist weed of waste ground, and undoubtedly the prettiest, growing to 90cm (3ft), with veined pink flowers. It has a spectacu-lar form called *M. sylvestris mauritiana* which, although slightly less hardy, can grow twice as big and has sump-tuous velvety flowers. All the mallow

species are summer-flowering. **Size** S: 45–60cm/1½–2ft. **Aspect** Full sun. **Hardiness** Hardy. **Soil** Any. **Propagation** Seed; cuttings. **Distri-bution** Europe. **Planting partners** Blue and purple wild flowers, such as *Geranium pratense*.

Meadowsweet see *Filipendula*

Michaelmas daisy see *Aster*

Milkweed see *Asclepias*

Mist flower see *Eupatorium*

Monarda
(Bergamot, bee balm)

Unrivalled for bold splashes of late summer colour in meadow or prairie plantings, monardas are rewarding plants. Bee balm (*M. didyma*) has scarlet flowers, wild bergamot (*M. fistulosa*) is pale lilac, with many culti-vars in a rich range of purples and reds. **Size** H: 90cm/3ft; S: 45cm/1½ft. **Aspect** Full sun. **Hardiness** Fully hardy. **Soil** *M. didyma* needs a damp soil; *M. fistulosa* is better on dry sites. **Propagation** Division; seed; spring cuttings. **Distribution** North Amer-ica; introduced to gardens elsewhere. **Planting partners** Yellow *Rudbeckia* and goldenrods (*Solidago*). Joe pye weeds (*Eupatorium*) and ironweeds (*Vernonia*) like similar conditions and so make good partners.

Obedient plant
see *Physostegia virginiana*

Monarda fistulosa
(wild bergamot)

Oenothera
(Evening primrose, sundrops)

The paper-thin petals of evening prim-rose are a source of constant delight in summer. They are mostly aggressively spreading flowers, ideal for weedy places and meadows. The best are white evening primrose (*O. speciosa*) and yellow sundrops (*O. fruticosa*). **Size** H and S: 30–75cm/1–2½ft. **Aspect** Full sun. **Hardiness** Fully hardy. **Soil** Any well-drained. **Prop-agation** Seed. **Distribution** Europe; North America. **Planting partners** Mallows (*Malva*), knapweeds (*Cen-taurea*), *Coreopsis*.

Ox-eye see *Heliopsis helianthoides*

Ox-eye daisy
see *Leucanthemum vulgare*

Oxlip see *Primula*

Phlox

This species comprises a large group of wild flowers, including some that are well known as garden flowers and many that are useful in wilder gardening. Summer phlox (*P. paniculata*) and carolina phlox (*P. carolina*) are two of several species that grow to around 90cm (3ft) high, flowering from mid- to late summer. These larger species do best in fertile soil and a slightly shaded aspect. There is also a good variety of smaller, spring-flowering species that thrive in shady woodland conditions and acidic soils. Blue phlox (*P. divaricata*) and creeping phlox (*P. stolonifera*) grow to around 20–30cm (8–12in) and spread well, to 45cm (1½ft) at least. The latter is particularly good as ground cover. Phloxes vary considerably in colour; each species often has cultivars in shades of pink, lavender, white and pale blue. **Hardiness** All the above are hardy. **Soil** Any fertile soil, but see above. **Propagation** Division; seed. **Distribution** North America; gardens elsewhere. **Planting partners** Cranesbills (*Geranium*) for the taller species and *Dicentra* for the smaller.

Polemonium
caeruleum
(jacob's ladder)

Physostegia virginiana

(Obedient plant, false dragonhead)
The obedient plant, named for the ease with which the bright pink, late summer flowers may be rearranged on the stem, is anything but obedient in the garden. Its rapidly spreading roots are a menace in the border but welcome in a truly wild garden.
Size H: 60–90cm/2–3ft; S: 90cm/3ft. **Aspect** Sun or part-shade. **Hardiness** Fully hardy. **Soil** Damp. **Propagation** Division; seed. **Distribution** North America; gardens elsewhere. **Planting partners** Strong-growing summer wetland plants like loosestrife (*Lythrum salicaria*), joe pye weeds (*Eupatorium*), ironweeds (*Vernonia*), irises.

Polemonium caeruleum

(Jacob's ladder)
A fine meadow plant, jacob's ladder has lavender-blue flowers in mid-summer and seeds itself around freely. *P. caeruleum album* is white.
Size H: 30–90cm/1–3ft; S: 45cm/1½ft. **Aspect** Sun. **Hardiness** Hardy. **Soil** Any well-drained. **Propagation** Seed. **Distribution** Europe; related species in North America.
Planting partners Looks good with pale pink musk mallow (*Malva moschata*), purple knapweeds (*Centaurea*) and pink cranesbills (*Geranium*).

Primula

(Primrose, cowslip, oxlip)
The primrose (*P. vulgaris*) is a much loved messenger of spring and a most rewarding wild flower to grow, its pale yellow flowers lighting up areas of woodland in steadily increasing numbers. Cowslips (*P. veris*) are even more prolific, with deeper yellow flowers in late spring, preferring more open conditions. The oxlip (*P. elatior*) has pale yellow flowers on a long stalk.
Size H: 10–15cm/4–6in; S: 15–30cm/6–12in. **Aspect** Light shade; cowslips prefer sun. **Soil** Any well-drained but not too dry. **Propagation** Division; seed is prolific but very slow, taking a year to germinate. **Distribution** All species mentioned, Europe. **Planting partners** Small spring flowers such as dwarf *Narcissus*, *Anemone* and violets (*Viola*).

Prunella vulgaris

(Self-heal)
One of the toughest and most adaptable small wild flowers, the rich, purple blooms of self-heal last most of the summer. Best grown with other small plants, in a wild flower lawn for instance, it spreads rapidly.
Size H: 10–30cm/4–12in; S: 30cm/1ft. **Aspect** Sun or part-shade. **Hardiness** Fully hardy. **Soil** Any fertile. **Propagation** Division; seed. **Distribution** Europe; Asia; introduced to

North America. **Planting partners** Small plants such as daisies (*Bellis*), clovers (*Trifolium*), birdsfoot trefoils (*Lotus*), bugles (*Ajuga*).

Purple coneflower
see *Echinacea purpurea*

Queen of the prairie see *Filipendula*

Ragged robin, rose campion
see *Lychnis*

Ranunculus

(Buttercup, lesser celandine, spearwort, fair maid of france)
Familiar yellow wild flowers in most temperate regions of the globe, there are some buttercups that are best regarded as weeds, but many to be encouraged as well. The lesser celandine (*R. ficaria*) is a small (8–15cm/ 3–6in), rapidly spreading flower of early spring with bright, glossy yellow flowers; it prefers shade and will grow in grass. The meadow buttercup (*R. acris*) is one of the most common, easy to establish in any sunny site; it has yellow flowers in early to mid-summer and grows 20–45cm/8in–1½ft tall. Another meadow species, somewhat larger (45–75cm/1½–2½ft) and flowering in early summer, is the lovely white fair maid of france (*R. aconitifolius*). The greater spearwort (*R. lingua*) is 1.5m (5ft) tall and spreads rampantly along ditches and pond margins, producing its yellow flowers in early summer.
Size S: equal to height (see above). **Aspect** Sun. **Hardiness** Fully hardy.

Soil Any, preferably moist. **Propagation** Division; seed. **Distribution** Europe; introduced to North America where there are also related species. **Planting partners** Other fast-growing, early summer flowering plants, violet and purple flowers.

Rudbeckia

(Black-eyed susan, coneflower)
Rudbeckias would definitely be in my top five wild flowers for the garden. They are easy, vigorous and flower prolifically for months in late summer and autumn. Black-eyed susan (*R. fulgida*) and its cultivar 'Goldsturm' form compact plants 45–75cm (1½–2½ft) high, with masses of rich, yellow flowers, each with contrasting dark centres, ideal for the border. *R. hirta* is very similar, and though it is not reliably perennial, it makes a good meadow wild flower. The thin-leaved coneflower (*R. triloba*) is a taller species, 60cm–1.5m (2–5ft), with similar flowers, whose leaves disappear beneath a blaze of yellow and black.
Size S: 60cm/2ft. **Aspect** Sun or a little shade. **Hardiness** Fully hardy. **Soil** Fertile, well-drained. **Propagation** Division; seed. **Distribution** North America; gardens in Europe. **Planting partners** Tall grasses, *Aster*, bergamots (*Monarda*), ironweeds (*Vernonia*).

Scabiosa

(Scabious)
Scabious provide some of the best mid- to late summer meadow flowers, and are sought after by butterflies. Small scabious (*S. columbaria*) has pale

Scabiosa columbaria (small scabious)

lavender pincushion flowers on 20–75cm (8in–2½ft) stems for months. Field scabious (*Knautia arvensis*) has similar flowers on taller, 30–90cm (1–3ft) stems while macedonian scabious (*K. macedonica*) has flowers of an extraordinary dark mauve-pink.
Size S: 30cm/1ft. **Aspect** Full sun. **Hardiness** Fully hardy. **Soil** Prefers dry, limy soils. **Propagation** Seed. **Distribution** Europe. **Planting partners** Knapweeds (*Centaurea*), meadow cranesbill (*Geranium pratensis*), evening primroses (*Oenothera*), mignonettes (*Reseda*).

Scabious see *Scabiosa*

Self-heal see *Prunella vulgaris*

Trifolium pratense
and *T. repens* (red
and white clover)

Silene

(Campion, fire-pink)

This varied group of colourful wild flowers generally blooms in late spring and early summer. Red campion (*S. dioica*) is, in fact, a deep pink and a superb plant, very easy and adaptable to a wide range of conditions such as meadows, hedgerows and light woodland; it also seeds itself around with gay abandon. White campion (*S. alba*) is a little less vigorous. Fire-pink (*S. virginica*) is a stunning, crimson, woodland species, flowering in spring. **Size** H: 30–60cm/1–2ft; S: 45cm/1½ft. **Aspect** Light shade or sun. **Hardiness** Fully hardy. **Soil** Any well-drained. **Propagation** Division; seed; cuttings. **Distribution** Europe; North America. **Planting partners** Bluebells (*Hyacinthoides non-scripta*), white stichworts (*Stellaria*), cow parsley (*Anthriscus sylvestris*) and other related plants such as sweet cicely (*Myrrhis odorata*).

Snakeroot see *Eupatorium*

Solidago

(Goldenrod)

There is a bewildering number of goldenrod species. They are nearly all large and vigorous, although there are a few dwarf species and cultivars around. As occupiers of difficult, weedy terrain and carriers of sunshine on dull, autumn days they are unrivalled. The best garden species are those that stay in one place, without spreading aggressively; sweet goldenrod (*S. odora*), seaside goldenrod (*S. sempervirens*), elm-leaved goldenrod (*S. ulmifolia*) and the only non-golden one, the creamy silver rod (*S. bicolor*). For meadow and prairie plantings or rough areas, the more thuggish species – canada goldenrod (*S. canadensis*), tall goldenrod (*S. altissima*) and late goldenrod (*S. gigantea*) – are useful. All flower from late summer into early autumn, and attract butterflies.
Size H: 75cm–1.5m/2½–5ft; S: 60cm/2ft. **Aspect** Sun or light shade. **Hardiness** Fully hardy. **Soil** Any well-drained. **Propagation** Division; seed. **Distribution** North America; introduced to Europe. **Planting partners** Complemented by tall, dramatic grasses such as bluestem (*Andropogon*) and mauve/purple flowers like *Aster* and ironweeds (*Vernonia*). Grow naturally with joe pye weeds (*Eupatorium*) and *Rudbeckia*.

Spearwort see *Ranunculus*

Spurge see *Euphorbia*

Stellaria

(Stitchwort, giant chickweed)

The chickweed's pure white spring flowers have a subtle beauty and complement brighter coloured flowers. The lesser and greater stitchworts (*S. graminea* and *S. holostea*) have a scrambling habit and should be kept to wilder parts of the garden. Giant chickweed (*S. pubera*) forms a tidier clump. **Size** H: 15–30cm/6–12in; S: 45–60cm/1½–2ft. **Aspect** Shade or half-shade. **Hardiness** Fully hardy. **Soil** Well-drained, moist. **Propagation** Seed; division. **Distribution** Europe; North America. **Planting partners** Campions (*Silene*), bluebells (*Hyacinthoides non-scripta*).

Stitchwort see *Stellaria*

Succisa pratensis

(Devil's bit scabious)

A bushy habit and a good supply of blue-purple, button-shaped flowers in mid- to late summer make this an excellent wild flower for borders, meadows and hedgerows.
Size H: 60–90cm/2–3ft; S: 45cm/1½ft. **Aspect** Sun or half-shade. **Hardiness** Fully hardy. **Soil** Any well-drained soil. **Propagation** Division; seed. **Distribution** Europe. **Planting partners** Other scabious, knapweeds (*Centaurea*), later flowering yellow daisies like *Rudbeckia*.

Sundrops see *Oenothera*

Tickseed see *Coreopsis*

Trifolium
(Clover)

Besides being pretty and good bee plants, clovers play an important part in meadow ecology, the nodules in their roots putting nitrogen into the soil. Red clover (*T. pratense*), which has pinky flowers, and the slightly smaller, white clover (*T. repens*) make fine additions to the wild flower lawn, flowering all summer. There are also agricultural clovers that are far too vigorous to grow with wild flowers, so they should be avoided.
Size H: 10–30cm/4–12in; S: 20–30cm/ 8–12in. **Aspect** Sun. **Hardiness** Fully hardy. **Soil** Any well-drained. **Propagation** Seed, best soaked in very hot water to soften. **Distribution** Europe; introduced to North America. **Planting partners** Small meadow wild flowers like self-heal (*Prunella vulgaris*), daisies (*Bellis perennis*) and germander speedwell (*Veronica chamaedrys*).

Trout lily see *Erythronium*

Vernonia
(Ironweed)

Almost ignored by the horticultural trade until recently, ironweeds have wonderfully rich purple flowers from late summer until well into the autumn. They thrive in damp meadow or prairie plantings and cope well with weeds. New york ironweed (*V. novebor-acens*) is the best known, but there are many similar species.
Size H: 1.5–2.5m/5–8ft; S: 45cm/ 1½ft. **Hardiness** Fully hardy. **Soil**

Prefer damp soil. **Propagation** Division; fresh seed. **Distribution** North America. **Planting partners** Yellow flowers like goldenrods (*Solidago*), *Rudbeckia* and sunflowers (*Helianthus*).

Vetch see *Vicia*

Vicia
(Vetch)

Vetches are summer-flowering members of the pea family that climb through other meadow plants by means of tendrils. Tufted vetch (*V. cracca*) is one of the most colourful, with dense flowerheads of pink-mauve. Common vetch (*V. sativa*) has larger mauve flowers. In addition, the closely related wild sweet peas (*Lathyr-us*) are a colourful group of wild flowers with a similar habit.
Size Vetches sprawl and climb to 2m/6½ft. **Aspect** Sun. **Hardiness** Fully hardy. **Soil** Any well-drained. **Propagation** Seed, soaked in very hot water before sowing. **Distribution** Europe; North America. **Planting partners** Grasses (to climb up!) and any other meadow wild flowers.

Viola
(Violet, wild pansy)

Sorting out the innumerable species of almost identical *Viola* is a botanist's nightmare. But they can be the wild flower gardener's dream, flourishing and flowering freely in shady places, and seeding themselves around happily. Most flower in spring, but there are some that will flower almost all

Silene dioica (red campion)

year round. Two notable species are sweet violet (*V. odorata*), one of several with a good scent, and wild pansy or heartsease (*V. tricolor*) which prefers sun and seeds rapidly, each offspring having slightly different flowers.
Size H: 5–15cm/2–6in; S: 15–30cm/ 6–12in. **Aspect** Most prefer shade, but will take sun if not too dry. **Hardiness** Fully hardy. **Soil** Any well-drained. **Propagation** Division; seed; cuttings. **Distribution** Europe; North America. **Planting partners** Violets look wonderful in woods in the early spring when seen with primroses (*Primula vulgaris*) and *Anemone*.

Violet see *Viola*

Wild carrot see *Daucus carota*

Wild pansy see *Viola*

Yarrow see *Achillea millefolium*

Index

Acknowledgments

Author's acknowledgments

There are many people one is indebted to in writing a book of this kind, either through direct contact or through books they have written which prove an invaluable source of reference. Many gardeners with wild flowers have been very helpful and I have learned much from listening to other people's experiences. The most detailed guides for wild flower gardening in Britain are John Stevens' *The National Trust Book of Wild Flower Gardening* (Dorling Kindersley) and Violet Stevenson's *The Wild Garden* (Windward). The value of gardens to wildlife is a major concern for most wild flower gardeners and the classic book on this subject is Chris Baines' *How to Make a Wildlife Garden* (Elm Tree Books).

I much appreciate the help of the team at the book's publisher, Conran Octopus; they have been an absolute delight to work with. Lastly, I owe much to my friend Jo Eliot, for her constant support.

Publisher's acknowledgments

The publisher would like to thank the following photographers and organizations for their kind permission to reproduce the photographs in this book:

1 John Glover; 2–3 Noel Kavanagh; 4–5 John Feltwell/Wildlife Matters; 6–7 John Feltwell/Wildlife Matters; 8 left Hugh Palmer; 8 right Ken Druse; 9 Michael Busselle; 10 Marijke Heuff (Priona Gardens, Holland); 11 left Jo Eliot; 11 right Andrew Lawson (Magdalen College); 12–13 Judy Glattstein; 14–15 Tania Midgley (Weeks Farm, Kent); 16 S & O Mathews (Stitches Farm House); 17 Marijke Heuff (Priona Gardens, Holland); 18 Hugh Palmer (East Lambrook Manor); 19 above Susan Witney; 19 below Annette Schreiner; 21 Photos Horticultural; 24 A–Z Botanical Collection; 25 Marijke Heuff (Priona Gardens, Holland); 27 above Brigitte Thomas; 27 below Marianne Majerus; 28 left Noel Kavanagh (Glen Chantry, Essex); 28 right Jerry Harpur (Great Dixter, Sussex); 30 Marijke Heuff/Garden Picture Library; 31 Annette Schreiner; 32 Jacqui Hurst (Great Warley Park, Essex); 33 Clive Nichols (Abbotswood Garden, Gloucestershire); 35 above Andrew Lawson (Hadspen House); 35 below Hugh Palmer; 36 Ken Druse; 37 Heather Angel; 39 above Annette Schreiner; 39 below A–Z Botanical Collection; 40 Zara McCalmont/Garden Picture Library; 41 Michele Lamontagne; 42–3 John Feltwell/Wildlife Matters; 44 Annette Schreiner; 45 John Heseltine; 47 above Michael Busselle; 47 below John Feltwell/Wildlife Matters; 48 Gary Rogers; 49 Heather Angel; 50 Jerry Harpur/Elizabeth Whiting & Associates; 51 Eric Crichton; 52 Ken Druse; 53 Judy Glattstein; 54 left Noel Kavanagh (The Beth Chatto Gardens); 54 right A–Z Botanical Collection; 55 Noel Kavanagh (Westwick Cottage); 56 above Noel Kavanagh (The Beth Chatto Gardens); 56 below Clive Nichols (Dartington Hall Garden, Devon); 57 John Glover (Little Wakestowe, Sussex); 58 above Gary Rogers; 58 below Susan Witney; 59 Tommy Candler; 60 Heather Angel; 61 Gary Rogers/Garden Picture Library; 62 Heather Angel; 63 Michele Lamontagne; 64 Georges Lévêque; 65 Heather Angel; 66 Annette Schreiner; 67 Heather Angel; 68–9 Jacqui Hurst (The Old Stores, Suffolk); 71 Susan Witney; 73 Michael Busselle; 75 Judy Glattstein; 76 Andrew Lawson (Chatsworth); 79 Andrew Lawson (Wisley); 83 Roger Hyam/Garden Picture Library; 84 Jacqui Hurst (Sawyer's Farm, Suffolk); 87 Andrew N. Gagg/Photos Flora; 89 Noel Kavanagh (The Magnolias, Essex); 93 Brigitte Thomas; 97 Marijke Heuff (Priona Gardens, Holland); 99–101 John Feltwell/Wildlife Matters; 102–3 Boys Syndication; 104 Clive Nichols (Painswick Rococo Garden); 105 Andrew Lawson; 106 John Heseltine; 107 Jacqui Hurst; 108–9 Michael Busselle; 110 Elizabeth Whiting & Associates; 112 A–Z Botanical Collection; 113 Harry Smith Collection; 114 Geoff Dann/Garden Picture Library; 116 John Glover; 117 A–Z Botanical Collection; 118 S & O Mathews; 119 Ken Druse; 120–1 Harry Smith Collection; 122 Heather Angel.

The publisher also thanks Helen Ridge, Barbara Nash and Janet Smy.

Index compiled by Indexing Specialists, Hove, East Sussex BN3 2DJ.